the
ART
of
WINE

the
ART
of
WINE

BY BABS HARRISON

⊞

PHOTOGRAPHS BY JEAN-MICHEL BERTRAND

COURAGE
B O O K S

An Imprint of Running Press
Philadelphia · London

NINETEENTH CENTURY TASTEVIN

© 2001 by Running Press
Photographs © 2001 by Jean-Michel Bertrand

All rights reserved under the Pan-American and International Copyright Conventions
Printed in China

This book may not be reproduced in whole or in part, in any form or by any means, electronic or mechanical, including photocopying, recording, or by any information storage and retrieval system now known or hereafter invented, without written permission from the publisher.

9   8   7   6   5   4   3   2
Digit on the right indicates the number of this printing

Library of Congress Cataloging-in-Publication Number 2001087018

ISBN 0-7624-1106-6

Cover and interior design by Rosemary Tottoroto
Edited by Victoria Hyun
Typography: Bembo and Binkham Script

This book may be ordered by mail from the publisher.
But try your bookstore first!

Published by Courage Books, an imprint of
Running Press Book Publishers
125 South Twenty-second Street
Philadelphia, Pennsylvania 19103-4399

Visit us on the web!
www.runningpress.com

Thank you to Bo Simons at The Sonoma County Wine Library,
collector Don Bull for sharing his time and stories,
Kerry Tessaro for being magical,
and Jennifer Worick and Victoria Hyun at Running Press.

And last but not least, many thanks to Robert McGarvey
for spiriting me away to wine country.
— Bab Harrison

I would like to thank the following people for giving me
access to their collection or their property:
⊞ Mr. François Labet and his parents, Château de la Tour, Vougeot, Burgundy
⊞ Mr. Claude Carlier, Château du Clos de Vougeot, Vougeot, Burgundy
⊞ Mr. Jèrôme Allexant, Marchè aux vins, Beaune, Burgundy
⊞ Mr. Devaux and Mr. Loic Riboteau, Cave du Patriache, Beane, Burgundy
⊞ Madame de Lenguesaing, Ms. Fabienne Durou nad Ms. Mariette Gouiaud,
Château Pichon Lonqueville Comtesse de Lalande, Pauillac, Mèdoc
⊞ Mr. Alain Querre, Musèe des Hospices de la Madeleine, St. Emilion
⊞ Ms. Nicole Feytou, Cave du Clos des menuts, St. Emilion
All images in are mine with the exception of images provided by Baccarat and Mercier.
All corkscrew photos: Don Bull/Jean-Michel Bertrand
— Jean-Michel Bertrand

CONTENTS

PAINTING FEATURING A BARREL MADE BY CHAMPAGNE MERCIER

FOR THE UNIVERSAL EXHIBITION OF 1889 IN PARIS.

Mercier advertising poster: Woman in Blue

Opposite: Decorative matchbox in polychrome metal

Introduction

As long as the world has had a pulse, there has been wine to fuel the ongoing story of civilization. Bottled water better hydrates our bodies, coffee more quickly snaps the brain awake, and cocktails spear all the good garnishes, but nothing inspires the soul and mind, or sparks the dying art of conversation, as well as the art of wine. While this vital beverage has existed since 5,000 B.C., America's voracious palate for fine wine has developed only in the last few decades, due in large part to the increasing number of stunningly good wines being produced around the world.

A turning point came as a blind tasting held in Paris in 1976, which pitted Napa's best wines against French first growths. The deck was stacked: all the judges were French. But California wines won in several categories, much to the shock of French critics. After that, a new appreciation for our domestic product was born, as was an accompanying wine culture. We have become ever more savvy, asking for wine no longer by color, but by varietal, maker, vintage, and sometimes specific vineyard. We've come a long way from guzzling the fizzy, screw-top wines of the 60s to the 2000 Napa Valley Wine Auction where a high-tech millionaire bought a six-liter bottle of Screaming Eagle Cabernet Sauvignon (made at a boutique Napa Valley winery by a woman winemaker) for half-a-million dollars.

MERCIER ADVERTISING POSTER: AVIATION

Wine is today's sexy, hot commodity, packaged with an aura of artistic *joie de vivre* and a romantic history longer than any gossiper's grapevine. Wine clubs, tastings, and classes have all multiplied in an attempt to satisfy the thirsty curiosity of amateur oenophiles.

Concurrent with our increased enjoyment of wine is a growing fascination with the accoutrements that are part of the wine drinking experience. Ever the muse, wine has inspired artists from the beginning of time to transform the simple act of drinking into a ritual filled with beauty. Painters, sculptors, potters, weavers, cutlers, glassmakers, silversmiths, and artisans of every type were smitten. They decorated palace walls and temples with depictions of the grape harvest, and created beautiful drinking, serving, and storage vessels adorned with enchanting images of the vine. While the range of contemporary wine objects is impressive, it is the antique objects that are lusted after by collectors who are keen to snag the brightest Sheffield Plate wine bucket, the highest quality silver-mounted claret jug, or a patented corkscrew with rare japanned decoration.

This book is an introduction to that increasingly popular realm of wine antiques, talismans that remind us not only of wine's pleasures throughout the ages, but of a particular culture, giving us a sense of our place in time. With elegant silhouettes, sensuous ornamentation, and exquisite craftsmanship, these *objets d'art* easily capture an audience. Alternately made from pottery, glass, bronze, silver, gold, and other elements, they reflect the material culture of civilizations from the Sumerians in Mesopotamia, the ancient Greeks and Romans, Europe's Renaissance artists, Georgian England's best silver and crystal craftsmen, the mechanical inventions of the Industrial Age, and the Victorian artisans who dreamed up increasingly fancy pieces for the dining tables of the wealthy middle class.

Very little remains from the earliest days of wine, but objects from the eighteenth century, an especially fine time for drinking in Europe thanks to improved vinification and storage methods which invigorated the production of fine drinking and serving vessels, can be found at varying price points pegged to the market's supply and demand, and the item's provenance and condition. Wine antiques may be ferreted out at auction, flea markets, and antique shops, and seen in museums and private collections, some of which are available to view on-line via the Internet.

The Art of Wine will introduce you to the splendor of antique wine accessories, such as that most essential tool to the enjoyment of wine, the corkscrew, and tell you why it has become one of the most in-demand collectibles of the last five years. The wit and crafts-

Mercier advertising poster: Railroad

manship of these tools, coupled with the mechanical inventions, have gripped some addicts to the point where their collections number in the thousands.

The technique of decanting, a necessity in the seventeenth century and a ritual which has survived to this day, created a range of accessories that are highly collectible: silver-capped jugs, crystal decanters, pierced coasters, shiny silver funnels, bottle tags, and tiny bowls known as tastevins. This last piece, often in silver engraved with the owner's initials, was a cellar master or wine professionals' portable cup for tasting wine from the barrel.

We'll also take a look at wine coolers, cellarettes, and monteiths, as well as wine glasses from the seventeenth century on. The evolution of the wine glass reflects the scientific advancements in glassmaking as well as the reigning design style of the day. Finally, we'll take a peek at a collectible that's a fine starting point for anyone who wants to dip their toe into the wine pool: bottle stoppers.

The amalgamation of grape growing, winemaking, and the visual arts has produced one of the more pleasant pasttimes known to man—the art of wine. So, uncork a bottle, pour yourself a glass, and continue a centuries-old tradition. We hope this book will inspire a passion in you to become a collector, or at the very least, to surround yourself with good wine and beautiful things. Cheers!

DECORATIVE METAL NOTEBOOK IN POLYCHROME

A BASKET OF GRAPEVINE–HANDLE CORKSCREWS

Wine vessels

Wine carrier fashioned out of clay, eighteenth century

Opposite:Inside the cellar of "Chateau de la Tour" in Burgundy

Without vessels—bottles, casks, and the like—there would be no wine on your table tonight. Containers may seem humble but they also are a sine qua non *for the wide distribution of wine and that's why, soon after wine was invented, artisans got busy creating containers that would allow the delicious elixir to be transported. Better still, containers are a field day for collectors.*

Why? While grapes have been grown and wine produced in basically the same fashion for millennia, the vessels used to store and transport this happy elixir have evolved from ancient amphorae whose pictures are splashed across the pages of art history books to today's mass-produced bottles that are casually tossed out once emptied. Along the way, animal skins were called into use (and still played an important role in holding wine well into this century—think of Ernest Hemingway's characters tilting back their skins in *The Sun Also Rises*). Besides these macho skins, pretty much anything that could hold a liquid was at some time put into service as a wine container—the Chinese fashioned bronze into wine vessels, others used silver and gold, and of course wood and clay played their roles. Whether the wine of the era tasted better in bronze or clay, we'll never know. But while the wine got drunk over thousands of years, we collectors are left with the vessels, which is probably the better end of the deal considering what wine used to taste like back then.

POTTERY-STYLE CARAFE MADE IN THE NINETEENTH CENTURY

EIGHTEENTH-CENTURY WINE SERVICE

The sad fact is, only museums and rarified private collections can afford to collect wine antiquities unearthed from the early Sumerian, Egyptian, Greek, and Roman civilizations—the British Museum in London may hold the most dazzling collections and nowadays very few, if any, genuine antiquities go up for sale in public markets. But the brighter news is that there are plentiful collectibles to be pursued and, for the collector of vessels, it is a search that leads back to the beginnings of wine.

The earliest winemakers used primarily earthenware amphorae to store and ship their precious liquid. These tall, earthenware jugs sported two handles at the neck for easier portability, and a body that tapered to a point at the bottom so they could be nestled into the sand or earth, leaned against one another in a cellar for storage, or placed in a pyramid as part of a pharaoh's bounty for the afterlife. The Egyptian scribes scratched brief notes in the clay describing the type and quality of the wine inside, providing information much as wine labels do today.

A FIRST CENTURY B.C. AMPHORA

A LOOK INSIDE THE CLOS DES MENUTS' WINE CELLAR.

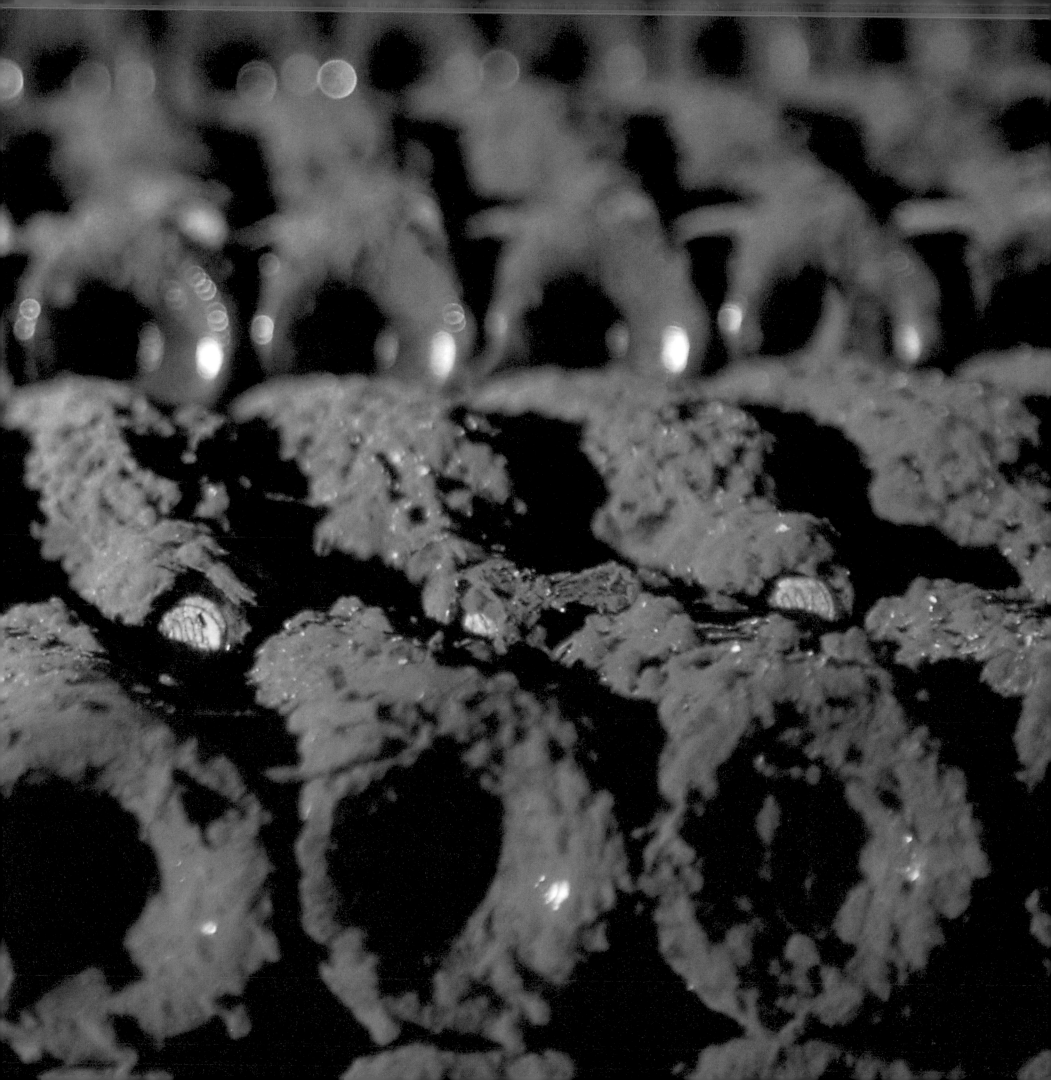

Hieroglyphics noting both the region where the grapes were grown and the vineyard have been found on Egyptian wine jars (many of which have recently been excavated by a joint Yale-Penn team working in Abydos, southern Egypt). Eventually, artisans began creating amphorae with flat bases, indicating the vessels were probably at that point stored on shelves.

The Greeks often coated the inside of their amphorae with pitch as a way to preserve the wine inside, and they sealed the top with more pitch and possibly terra cotta or grape leaves. To this day, Greeks retain a fondness for the pine flavor as evidenced by the distinctive Greek wine, Retsina. Their amphorae for home use were highly decorated with red or black figures, often depicting *symposia*—wine-infused gatherings where philosophers, artists, and statesmen would gather to recline, sip wine, converse, and be entertained—or images of satyrs with the gods, especially the Greek god of wine, Dionysus, a feisty spirit who, in addition to giving mankind both honey and wine, fought

Eighteenth-century french wine carrier

DISCOVERED IN FRANCE,
THIS SEVENTEENTH-
CENTURY VESSEL WAS
USED TO SERVE WINE

USED TO CARRY WINE
BY PILGRIMS ON THEIR
WAY TO ST. JACQUES
DE COMPOSTELLE.
THE SHELL'S SHAPE IS
TYPICAL OF ST. JACQUES.

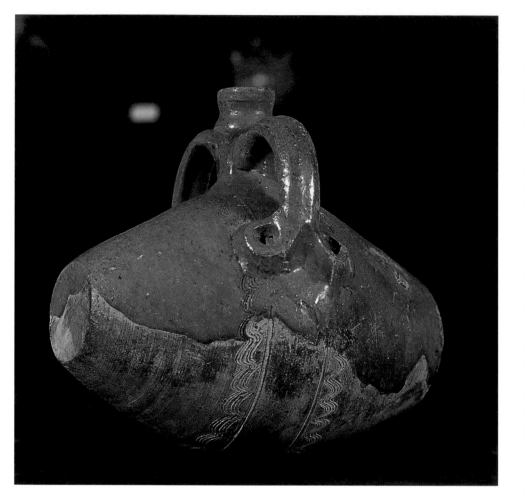

EIGHTEENTH-CENTURY WINE CARRIER MADE OUT OF CLAY

pitched battles as far from home as India and turned errant sailors into dolphins. (In later years, Dionysus morphed into the more jovial Roman god, Bacchus.) As the Greeks always diluted their wine, they would pour wine from an amphora into a *krater* (a two-handled urn), and add water from a pitcher. *Kyathos*, long-handled cups, were used to ladle out the wine into a *kylix*, a double-handed drinking cup.

Rare antiquities all, some vessels are still being discovered. An underwater archaeological expedition off the coast of Sicily in the fall of 2000 retrieved 300 earthenware amphorae, one of which was completely intact. It was dated to the mid-twelfth century, and held about four liters of Sicilian wine. The rescued amphora was still sealed with its original wax with a perfectly intact cork.

As early as the first century A.D., wine storage shifted to barrels, wooden containers said to have been invented in the Alps, according to the Roman historian Pliny the Elder. Many woods were used— Herodotus noted the transport of wine to Mesopotamia using barrels crafted of palm

THE INSIDE CELLAR OF PAYS D'OC

New and old bottles of champagne

EIGHTEENTH-CENTURY BOTTLE

SEGURA VIUDAS CHAMPAGNE

wood—but, eventually, the preferred wood became oak and barrel-making achieved maturity in the hands of Celtic and Gallic coopers.

By the Middle Ages, coopers were fashioning wood barrels for the shipping of wine to merchants, alehouses, and wealthy households, but it wasn't until the sixteenth century that someone also thought of aging wine in the barrel. Barrel sizes, too, varied—some supposedly could hold a million gallons—but nowadays most wine barrels have a more manageable capacity of 59 (the Bordeaux style) or 60 gallons (Burgundy).

Glass bottles were introduced in the seventeenth century, and collectors have been fascinated by the evolution of the wine bottle, from the first hand-blown, crudely bulbous shapes to the mass-produced, cylindrical form we are familiar with today. Another underwater archaeological find in the fall of 2000 brought to the surface a 350-year-old bottle of Portuguese wine recovered from a seventeenth-century Dutch warship. The green, onion-shaped bottle is among the oldest found to date with its cork and wine intact, and one of the earliest examples of a

WINE PRODUCED IN PAYS D'OC

INSIDE CLOS DES MENUTS' WINE CELLAR
IN ST. EMILION, FRANCE.
THE CELLAR WAS HAND CARVED
IN THE STONE BY MONKS

corked wine bottle.

In the early seventeenth century, glass containers were still a rarity, enjoyed only by the upper classes of society. Lower classes would have used leather or earthenware vessels for their wine. But for a gentleman, a "shaft and globe" style glass bottle, with a cork secured at the rim by a tied string, was the only way to serve wine at the table. These bottles were sometimes "wanded" with wicker or leather, as occasionally seen in paintings by Hogarth, probably for extra padding while traveling. The roundish base with tall neck is thought to have been designed for expert storage in sand beds on cellar floors.

These greenish glass bottles began sporting identifying marks or seals of the owner in the mid-seventeenth century, thanks to a British law of 1636 which forbade merchants to sell wine in bottles as a protection to the customer: bottles varied widely in size. Households were forced to buy their own bottles—some accounts listed as many as 500 in a year—and bring them to the vintner to be filled from a barrel. The bottle seal, an impression made by

1945 Chateau
de la Tour,
Clos Vougeot,
Burgundy

the glassblower, indicated the owner's initials and the year. It identified the bottle as theirs in a cellar that was probably filled with myriad green bottles, all similar in appearance. This mark, used until the Victorian age, provides a valuable form of provenance to collectors.

The wine bottle's cylindrical shape started taking form in the early eighteenth century when binning was introduced. It is partially due to port, which now was able to be imported from Portugal to Britain at lower rates of duty, thus increasing its popularity. The rogue wine needed to be aged and it was soon discovered that by lying the bottle on its side, keeping the cork wet and tight, the wine could mature in the bottle with little air seepage. This of course required a cylindrical-shaped bottle, a tighter cork, and a better instrument with which to remove it: the corkscrew.

Bottle molds were introduced in the next century, allowing for uniform size and mass production. Hand-blown glass and bottle seals were forgotten in a desire for speed and uniformity. In 1902, an American created an automatic bottle production machine able to produce 50,000 glass bottles a day. The disposable bottle had been born, yet continued to take on distinctive silhouettes that would indicate the region of origin of the liquid it carried: sloping shoulders for Burgundy, high shoulders for Bordeaux, and the long, slender bottles that are distinctive of Alsace.

"Le Patriarche"
wine cellar in
Beaune, Burgundy

Corkscrews

A 15-INCH, DOUBLE-LEVER CORKSCREW BASED ON

CIPRIANO GHIDINI'S 1973 AMERICAN DESIGN PATENT

OPPOSITE: "BARMAID": 1950S TO 1960S ITALIAN DOUBLE-LEVER CORKSCREW

Throughout history, corkscrews have been made to be provocative gems. While created essentially to perform a function—without corkscrews, wine would stay in its bottles, undrunk—corkscrew makers for centuries have been whimsical, artistic, and playful in interpreting just what a proper corkscrew should look like.

Many were ornamented with silver or gold; sheathed in sleek cases of shagreen (a distinctive, untanned leather) or elegant enamel, fashioned into the likenesses of noble animals or shapely women's legs; and crowned with decorations of plump grapes, cocked pistols, and salacious, grinning images of Dionysus, god of the vine and of joyous life. The corkscrew, the wine business' principal tool with a lengthy provenance and a singular purpose, has been described as "an instrument of common sense, with which obstacles on the path to enjoyment are removed."

This twisted instrument, crucial to Bacchanalian feasts and picnics in the grass, comes in many guises—elegant, precious, erotic, and pedestrian—and over a thousand patents have been awarded for the introduction of new and useful improvements. Almost four centuries after its invention, it still remains the best tool for extracting a tight cork, and in the process it has become a relatively recent hot collectible, even generating intense interest—and bidding—at auctions held by Christie's in London. Prices above $15,000 have recently been hit at auctions and insiders see no

Corkscrew knives in the shape of champagne bottles
with various advertisements for champagne producers

WAITERS' FRIEND

EARLY NINETEENTH-CENTURY DUTCH SILVER
TRAVELING CORKSCREW WITH LION-FIGURE HANDLE;
SHOWN WITHOUT PROTECTIVE SHEATH FOR WORM

"HOOTCH OWL": RICHARD SMYTHE'S
1936 AMERICAN-PATENT DOUBLE LEVER

diminution in enthusiasm for corkscrews. Christie's itself now holds two auctions yearly—which bring out throngs and trigger intense bidding—and competitive houses have entered into the action. Suddenly, corkscrew collecting is all the rage.

Why do people collect them in the first place? Curators say that collectors typically are on the hunt for pieces because of their artistry—either the elaborate designs or the mechanical functionality—but, *sotto voce*, they add that the real draw of corkscrew collecting is that it remains highly affordable, with pieces at auction sometimes selling for as little as $100 (and avid collectors say that good finds turn up at flea markets for as little as $5 or $10). Wine itself may be zooming into stratospheric financial reaches,

but certain corkscrews remain an object for the everyman to collect—and, certainly, they are doing just that nowadays.

Who would have guessed a simple turn of the screw would elicit such worldwide attention—and in Britain of all places, a country that does not even produce wine? Yet, London has become the epicenter (followed by New York) of the increasingly popular wine antiques business, and it is in this city traditionally known for its beers and ales that a *helixatrope* (corkscrew addict) has the best chance of checking off his list of desiderata and still finding more he hadn't known he wanted. Why London? The British capital has not only a long tradition of antiquing along Portobello Road and in smart shops tucked into

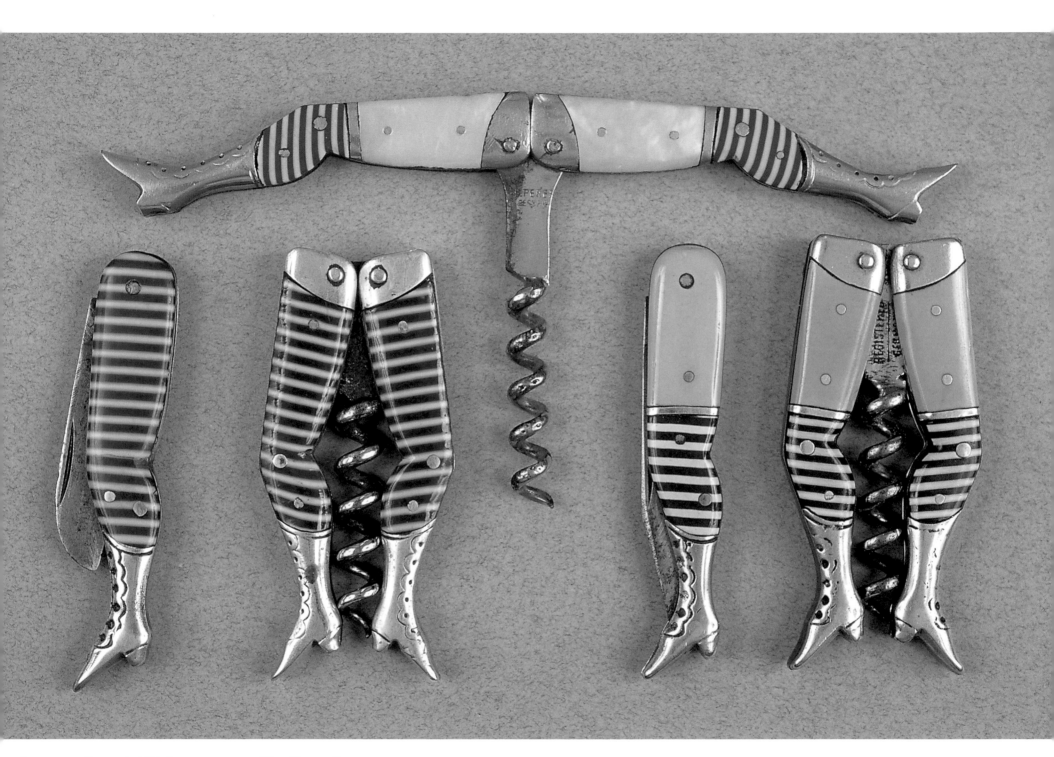

STEINFELD & REIMER'S 1894 GERMAN PATENTED "GAY NINETIES"
LEGS. THE LEGS WERE PRODUCED IN OVER 50 COLOR SCHEMES.
SETS INCLUDING MATCHING KNIVES ARE RARE.

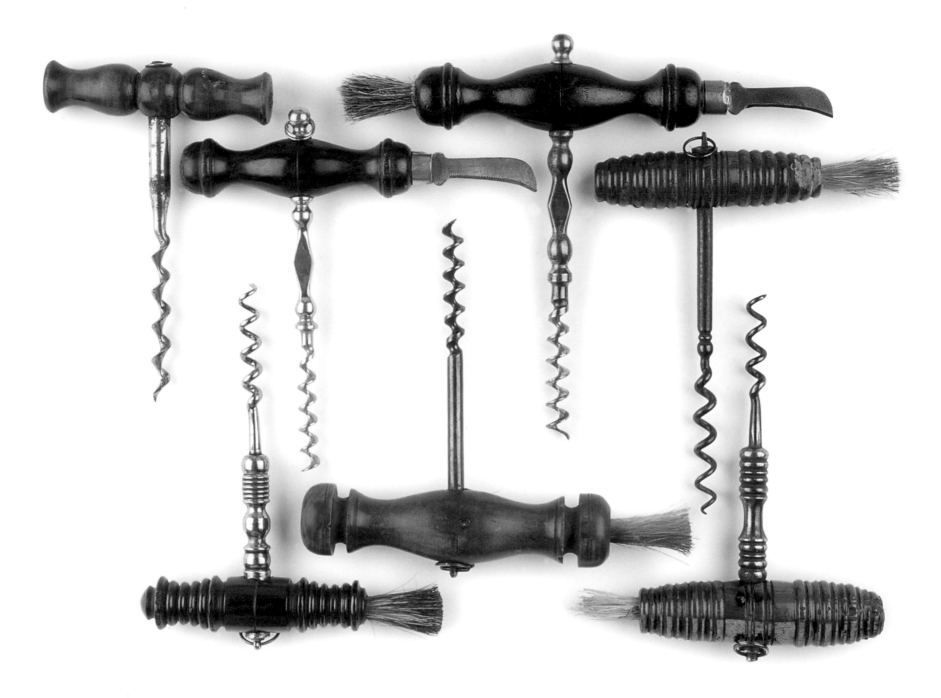

VARIOUS DIRECT-PULL WOOD-HANDLE CORKSCREWS, INCLUDING SOME WITH BRUSHES FOR CLEANING

CELLARED BOTTLES AND SOME WITH CUTTERS FOR REMOVING WAX OR LEAD SEALS

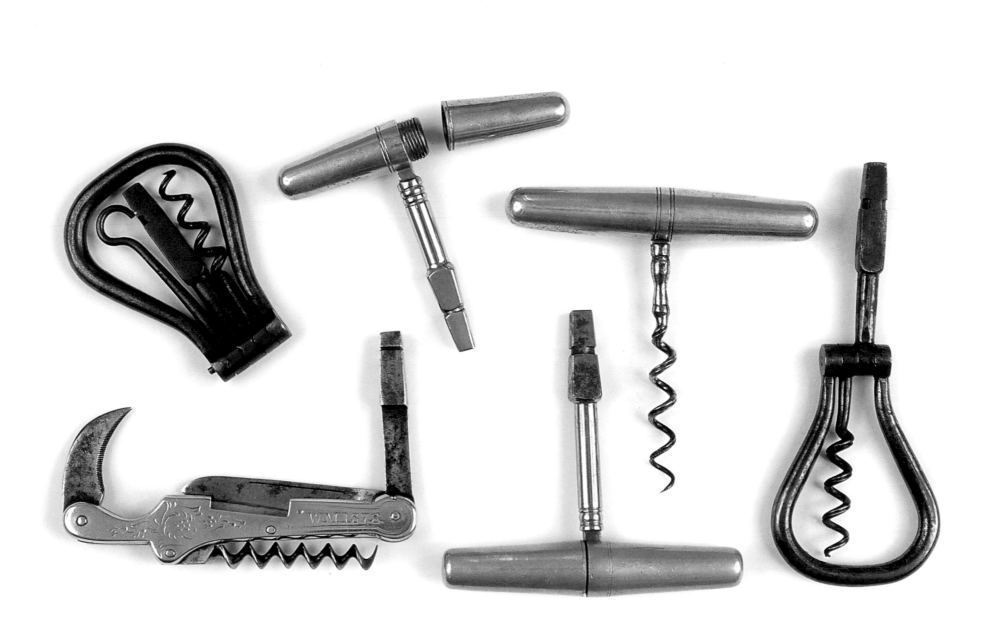

Two folding bows having several implements including a carriage key. A knife engraved "W.M. 1878" with a carriage key. Matching "roundlet" carriage key and corkscrew.

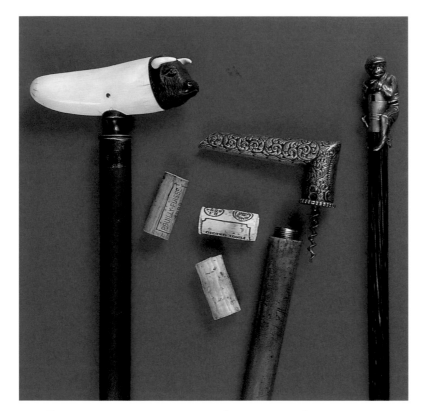

CORKSCREWS CONCEALED IN CANES. LEFT TO RIGHT: A MODERN CANE
WITH BULL-FIGURE HANDLE, A NINETEENTH-CENTURY SILVER-HANDLE CANE,
AND AN EARLY NINETEENTH-CENTURY MONKEY-HANDLE CANE

BOTTLE STOPPER WITH A COLLAR SPECIALLY MADE BY MOËT & CHANDON
TO AVOID LOSS OF GAS FROM CHAMPAGNE BOTTLES

"malls" throughout the city, but an even longer tradition of filling their bellies with wine. Britain also made quite a few elegant wine accessories in its time, including the corkscrew.

For collectors, the only real problem is how to narrow the hunt. With so many types of corkscrews to choose among, collectors have to decide if and how to focus their collection: will it be strictly English examples, or perhaps German; patented models, or just concertina mechanisms; silver and gilt examples, or exclusively horn and tusk pieces? Here's

how sharply focused corkscrew collecting can become: one enthusiast in coastal Florida acquires corkscrews with carved images of alligators. And he has hundreds! Not really as strange as it sounds: around the turn of the twentieth century, Florida enjoyed a tourist boom, visitors wanted something unique to take home to commemorate their stay, and crafty entrepreneurs soon began churning out corkscrews featuring likenesses of alligators. They flew off the shelves—and now, a century later, are flying into the sale bins at glitzy auction houses.

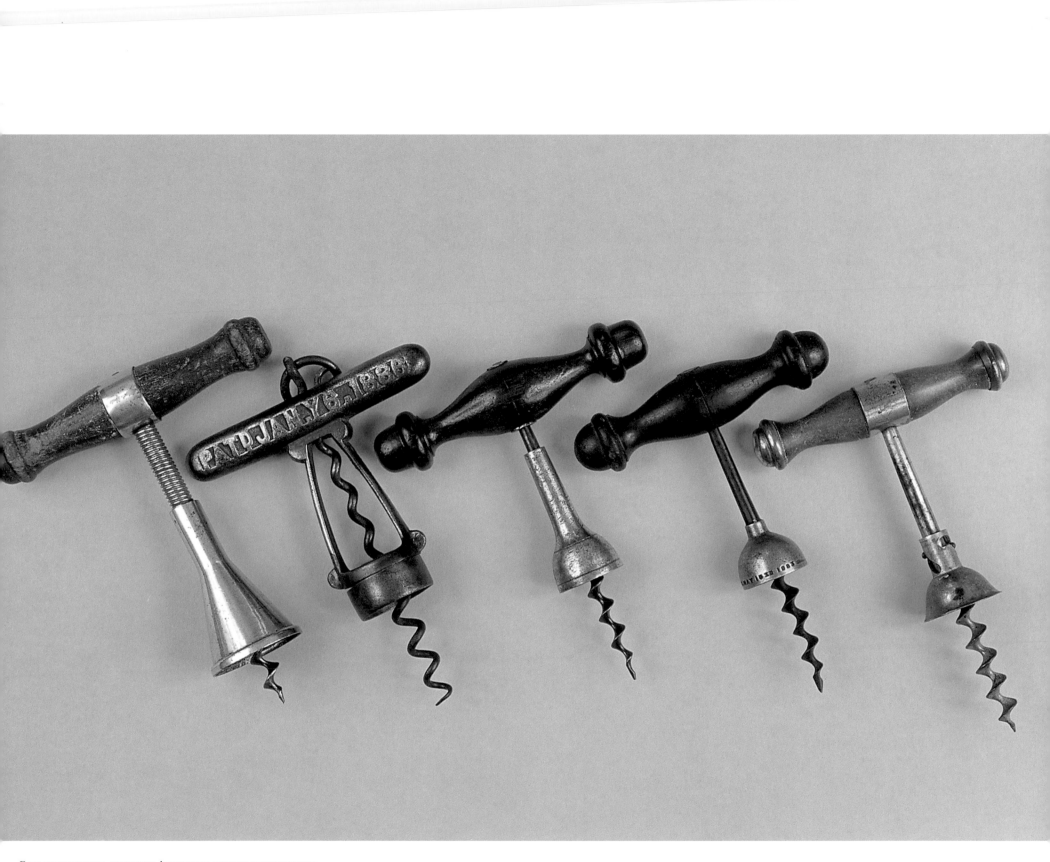

Five nineteenth-century American patent corkscrews.
Left to right: Strait (1883), Woodman (1886), Griswold
(1884), Bennit (1883), and Curley (1884).

PISTOLS WITH CORKSCREW TRIGGERS, BARRELS, AND SIGHTS

CORKSCREWS FOR THE GOLFER, INCLUDING AN AUSTRIAN DESIGN BY HAGENAUER

A RARE "EXPRESS" WAITER'S FRIEND WITH TIGER HEAD,
PRODUCED BY JACQUES PERILLE, PARIS

Turn of the Screw

Despite the vast array of styles, the corkscrew's essential bones have changed little over the centuries. Though it has evolved from a simple twist of wire with a finger pull to a complex mechanical instrument requiring little human strength, it remains essentially a three-part tool made up of handle, shaft, and worm.

The worm, the crucial element that bores into the potentially difficult cork, can be one of two types. The less popular is the Archimedian, named after the second century B.C. Greek mathematician, which takes the form of his famous water screw: a solid shank around which winds a sharpened worm. A drawback: this worm tends to chew into the cork and leave bits in the wine. That's why the other style, the Helix, is the more popular. It does less damage to a temperamental cork, and is a continuous spiral resembling a tight ringlet of hair, or tendril from an ivy plant.

The handle and shaft of the corkscrew offered *tabula rasa* to artists, who endowed these wine-related instruments with such perfect proportion and beauty, that even in their time they must have been regarded as small wonders. Sturdy handles have been created from smooth, silver-mounted horn curved sinuously over the shaft; gleaming ornamented steel; brass; silver; semi-precious stones such as agate; wood carved to resemble wine barrels; and reticulated antler, warthog tusk, or highly polished bone carved into fanciful forms such as whistling greyhound heads, crouching lions, and snorting bulls.

While no one knows the whereabouts of the very first wine corkscrew—might it repose in some obscure collection or lie

Early twentieth century postcard printed in Cuba advertising Bacardi Rum and beer. The waiter is using a direct-pull corkscrew to remove the cork from the bottle of rum.

"Cellar keys" with corkscrews hidden in the sheaths

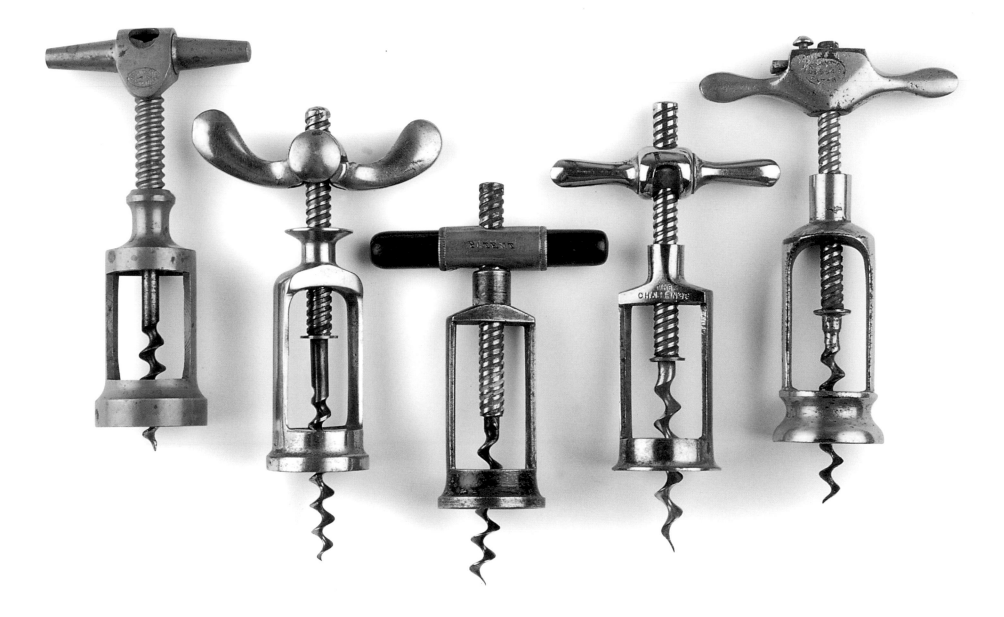

Open-frame corkscrews with handles which are "locked" to turn the worm
into the cork and "unlocked" to extract the cork.

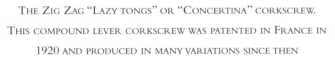
The Zig Zag "Lazy tongs" or "Concertina" corkscrew. This compound lever corkscrew was patented in France in 1920 and produced in many variations since then

beneath a sunken manor awaiting excavation by a crack archeological team—we can say that the earliest wine corkscrew was invented no earlier than the cork.

Cork is pulled from the inside bark of a cork oak, which does not even begin to take on a personality until it is a tree of uncertain age, about 50 years, at which point it can be stripped for cork only once every nine years. The best trees are said to grow in the Mediterranean-hugging region of Portugal. Cork is an ingenious stopper—it holds its shape without absorbing impurities, it expands and contracts to fit its allotted space, and the proper fit produces a leak-proof seal. In the early days, before the invention of the bottle cap, corks were the closure of choice for all liquids, not just wine. Cork is still used today, although some wineries are replacing it with a synthetic stopper (which still requires a corkscrew), or a screwtop (which doesn't), in hopes of alleviating the 7 percent incident rate of corked or musty wine.

The earliest corkscrew, or bottlescrew as it was then called, is believed to have been made by gunsmiths in the seventeenth

IRON CORKSCREWS

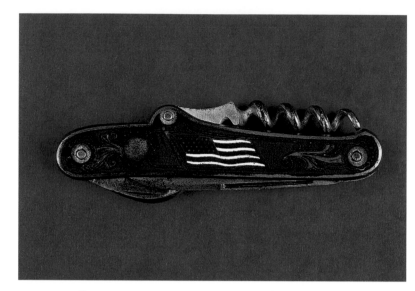

ENAMEL-HANDLE KNIFE DEPICTING THE AMERICAN FLAG.
PRODUCED IN GERMANY C.1900

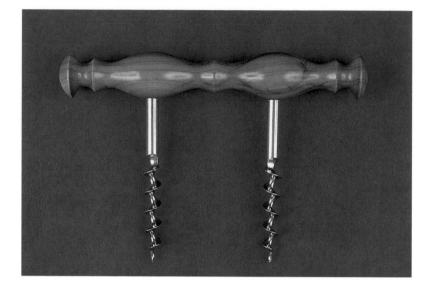

A LIMITED EDITION OF TWENTY OF THIS RIGHT-AND-LEFT-HAND WORM
CORKSCREW WAS PRODUCED IN STEINBACH-HOLLENBERG, GERMANY, IN THE 1990S

century who fashioned it after a double-helix instrument they used to remove wadding from gun barrels. As bulbous bottles slowly morphed into cylindrical ones that reclined, the cork also changed shape and was driven in all the way to provide a snugger fit in the now stronger bottleneck, thus requiring a tool beyond the human hand to remove it. Though rare in the early eighteenth century, a corkscrew would have been an ubiquitous tool by the end of it. A profession of cutlers arose, some of whom became known for their inventions and patents.

"The eighteenth century was a glorious period of corkscrew making," says Bert Giulian, author of *Corkscrews of the Eighteenth Century: Artistry in Iron and Steel*.

"The eighteenth century corkscrews are a legacy

of beauty, grace, and charm combined with exquisite, individual craftsmanship. They became an essential part of the gentleman's equipment, frequently carried on his person."

Portability was key to many of the early corkscrew designs, which were used to open perfume, ink, and medicine bottles in addition to wine. Popular styles included sheathed finger loop corkscrews, with the sheath sometimes doubling as a knife sharpener or pipe tamper (later in the century, the portable sheath became even more user-friendly when the sheath cunningly slipped into the finger loop to become a "T" handle, still a common form of corkscrew used today); the double-hinged shaft models, which folded to a third its length; and the folding bow or harp (the

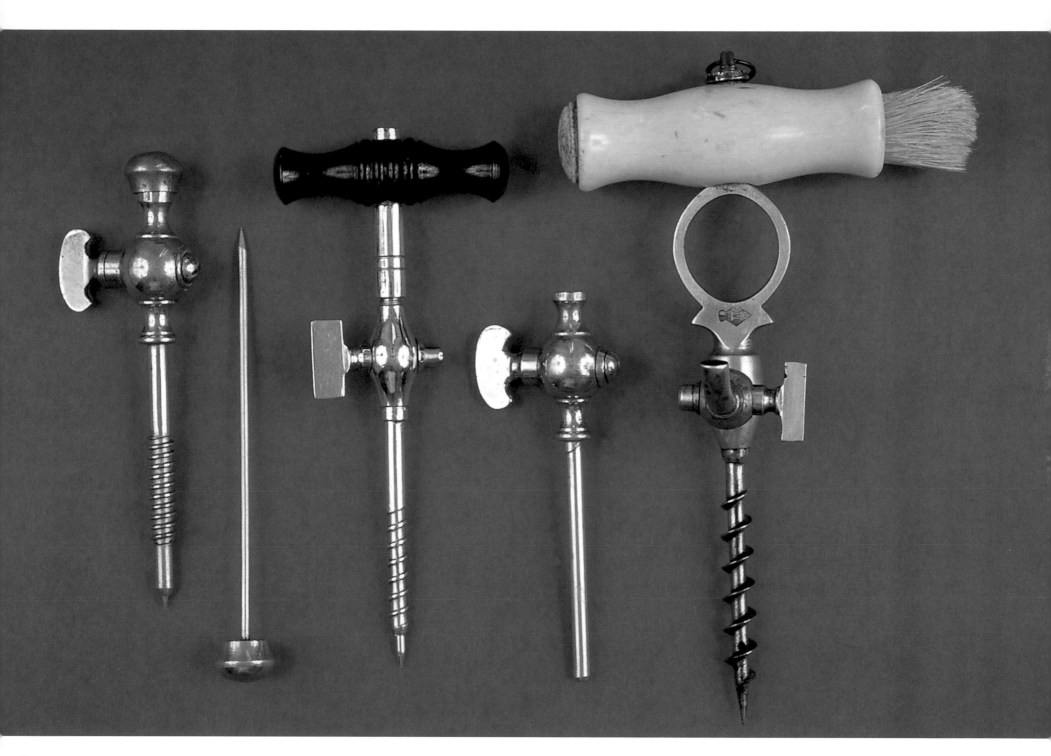

CHAMPAGNE OR SODA-WATER TAPS PENETRATE THE
CORK OF A BOTTLE, AND BY OPENING AND CLOSING A
VALVE, THE USER CAN DRAW OFF AS MUCH BUBBLY AS
DESIRED WITHOUT SPOILING THE CONTENTS

A Scottish couple with bakelite heads. Their costumes
are hand-painted on the leather sheaths

French versions are frequently heart–shaped), in which the handle folds over to protect the helix. Ingenious craftsmen would expand the folding bow's size to incorporate myriad useful tools. These combination corkscrews, forerunners of today's Swiss Army knife, might include a pipe cleaner, rasp, sewing needle, pricker, snuff shovel, tweezers, and a long auger, among other necessities.

While utility was certainly high on the list of wants in a corkscrew, design was not to be left behind, especially if left to the French. Gallic craftsmen busied themselves ornamenting "T" handle and finger pull corkscrews with carved fish, tortoise heads, bewitching swans, and other animal motifs. Ornamentation to the max seemed to be the order of the day for the French baroque style. Many examples feature exquisitely beautiful ornamentation in burnished or gilded steel, silver, tortoise-shell, and mother of pearl. Rosettes, grapevines, fleur de lis, lions, and unicorns, hearts, coats of arms, and monograms, pre-sumably those of the owner, ornamented these gorgeous tools which would have

TWO RARE SILVER-HANDLE CORK EXTRACTORS PATENTED
BY MACHIL CONVERSE IN THE UNITED STATES IN 1899

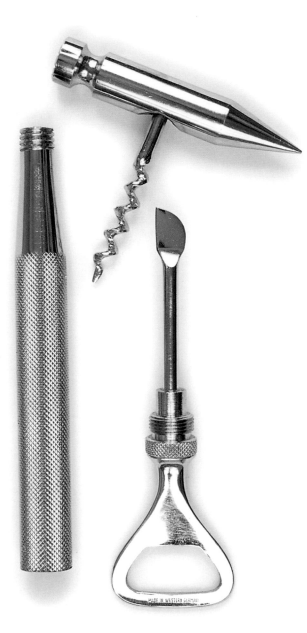

A German multi-tool including corkscrew, bottle-cap lifter, and ice pick

looked perfectly at home at any of France's great chateaux.

One especially beauteous creation is the French Cage (*tire-bouchon à cage*). Giulian dates them back to the seventeenth century, saying they were most commonly made of pierced steel. These are intricately cut cages, featuring openwork, balustered, and gadrooned ornamentation, rendering steel into an irresistably sensuous material. Only the French could have succeeded in giving this heavy metal such a stylish and feminine silhouette. The cages probably worked as good as they looked: turn the handle in one direction, and the cork is neatly lifted from the bottle through the cage. No doubt, the *tire-bouchon à cage* was a prized accessory of the wealthier nobles of France.

While the French were busy flirting with frilly designs, the British across the Channel were producing equally evocative corkscrews in heavy, masculine styles with good bones, as did the Irish, whose most important cutler was Thomas Read, whose signature model—called a "Read's Coaxer"—features a concave brass button between the helix and the shaft that "coaxes" the cork loose from the bottle when the two make contact. If you run across one, you've found a treasure.

The first corkscrew patent was awarded in 1795 to Reverend Samuel Henshall while an Anglo-Saxon scholar at Oxford, for a version very similar to Read's Coaxer with a concave button. Henshall's patent introduced a "button" placed between the worm and shank; when the button came in contact with the cork, it prevented the helix from turning any further and gave the cork enough of a nudge to help dislodge its

THE WOOD DOUBLE-ACTION CORKSCREW IS
SHOWN ON THE FRENCH POSTCARD ENTITLED,
"TRADITIONS DE JADIS—LE CHABROT."

tight seal. This style was extremely popular and England produced them for more than a century. Imprinted on each was a Latin proverb: *Obstando Promoves*—by standing firm, one makes advancement.

Patents for mechanical corkscrews flourished in the nineteenth century. The first corkscrew patent of the century was given to Sir Edward Thomason in 1802. His improvement allowed the worm to both enter the cork and remove it with a continuous turning of the handle. The corkscrew's efficiency subsequently was further improved upon with numerous patents introducing new means of leverage, torque, rack and pinion, and the use of gasses, all to more easily dislodge a little cork from a bottle. Each patent was registered, and the corkscrews produced often bear the mark of the year and the patent, an important mark for serious collectors.

This continuous reinvention of the corkscrew continues through to today, with probably the most famous contemporary patent being a 1980s creation called the Screwpull, patented by Houston oil drilling engineer Herbert Allen. His design featured

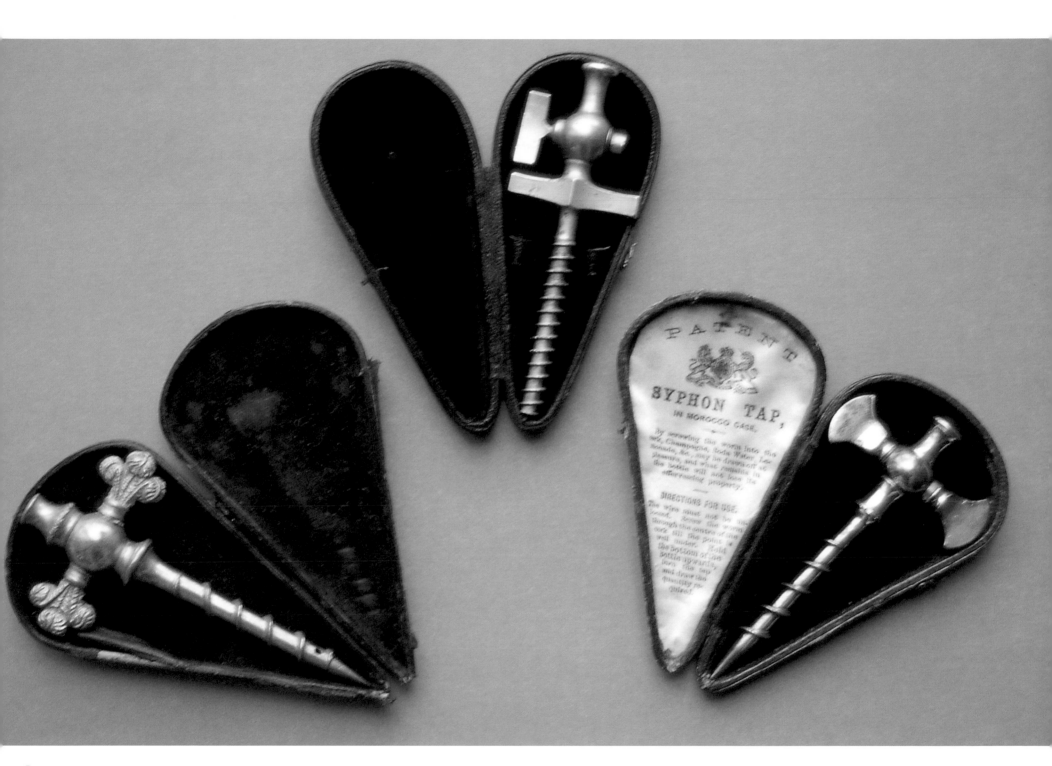

CHAMPAGNE OR SODA-WATER TAPS USED TO PENETRATE THE CORK AND
DRAW-OFF ONLY THE DESIRED AMOUNT WITHOUT SPOILING THE REST.

A FANCY FRENCH BOTTLE SEALER MARKED "L'EUREKA, BTE, S.G.D.G."
ON THE HANDLE LINK, AND "DOISTAU PARIS" ON THE COLLAR. BTE IS THE
ABBREVIATION FOR BREVETE, WHICH MEANS PATENT. S.G.D.G. IS AN
ABBREVIATION FOR SANS GARANTIE DU GOVERNEMENT, MEANING WITHOUT
THE GUARANTEE OF THE GOVERNMENT

THIS CORKSCREW HAS A FOIL CUTTER FOR REMOVING THE CAPSULE ON
THE BOTTLE TOP AND A BRUSH FOR REMOVING ANY RESIDUE

a 6-inch-long plastic clothespin-like tool with a 5-inch, Teflon-coated worm which has become a favorite of many aficionados for its sheer ease of use. But even Screwpull improved on its design when the company later introduced the Leverpull which removes a cork with even less effort and in less time.

The Art of Whimsy

Teflon is one thing, shapely women's legs and flap-ping owl's wings another. Where corkscrew creators really excel is in producing whimsical—but, always, still useful—models. Wildly collectible examples include the double-lever action "Hootch-Owl," patented by R.G. Smythe of Valley Stream, New York, in 1935. The metal owl's eyes are closed on one side but open on the reverse. The owl's wings, formed by the levers which also double as cap lifters, fly up as the cork is released. Turn-of-the-century

French flynut corkscrews

German "legs" work on the same principle, a woman's flesh-colored or colorfully striped celluloid legs with buttoned ankle boots rise as the cork is pulled. If the legs are half flesh and half striped—up to the knees—grab it, as it is particularly rare.

American-made corkscrews mastered the art of advertising, transforming a wooden handle on a simple T-shape corkscrew into the equivalent of today's T-shirt, promoting all makes of alcoholic spirits as a giveaway to customers. During Prohibition, "Old Snifter" came into production, a corkscrew that mimicked Senator Andrew Joseph Volstead, the author of the so-called Volstead Act that launched Prohibition. To use a Snifter, grab the Senator and turn his top hat. A worm peeks out behind his long coat. Covet one? So many of these politically pregnant corkscrews were made that, even today, prices remain low—rarely over $100 for one in good condition.

The Collectors

When does a person move from simply owning a few corkscrews to being a collector? Count up the corkscrews you own. If the total is under 100, keep buying. Most serious collectors—an ever increasing lot of addicts—have no fewer than 1,000 models laying around their house, tucked into cabinets and piled on desks.

"Corkscrew collecting has grown considerably over the last several years due to the wider availability of books on the subject, websites, and the growing interest in wine, which goes hand in hand with the corkscrew," says collector Don Bull,

A clown double lever based on designs by Carlo
Gemelli of Italy and produced in the 1950s and 1960s

owner of over 6,000 corkscrews. He is also the author of *The Ultimate Corkscrew Book* which features some of his ever-growing personal collection.

"I retired at 53 just so I could screw around," he jokes. Bull actually did retire early, probably to keep up with his enormous collection and website which documents his collection and provides links to other clubs and collectors. He's paid anywhere from $1 to $10,000 for a corkscrew, and he's still on the prowl for corkscrews he doesn't have and models he has never seen before. He credits e-Bay with driving prices down, wonderful for a buyer, but not so good for collectors who wish to sell. He remembers when German "legs" used to sell at Christie's semi-annual auctions for 300–400 pounds (around $450–$600). "Now you can find them on e-Bay for $200–$400," he says. "There are so many 'legs' walking out of closets and cupboards now, it's driving the prices down."

If you really want to join the premier corkscrew club, it's the ICCA. But you may have to wait your turn. The International Correspondence of Corkscrew Addicts was started in 1974 in London by the late Bernard Watney as a way for serious collectors to communicate their finds. It is limited to 50 members with extraordinary collections who research as well as collect corkscrews. They hold jubilant, annual meetings in Europe or in the U.S.

where they trade, buy, and search for more corkscrews, and exchange knowledge on an annual basis with the "best six examples" from their corkscrew collections accompanied with detailed notes. Don Bull is past "right" (presidents are called "right" following Henry Clay's statement that he'd rather be right than president). Brother Timothy, cellarmaster emeritus of the Christian Brothers Winery in Napa, California is the group chaplain. He amassed over 1,800 corkscrews which are now on display at the Culinary Institute of America's Greystone facility in Napa, which previously housed the Christian Brothers Winery.

With such limited membership and the rising interest in corkscrew collecting, it wasn't long before other clubs began forming. The Canadian Corkscrew Collectors Club (CCCC) was founded in 1981 and has an unlimited international membership, welcoming those who are interested in corkscrews and pay their annual dues (currently $30). CCCC claims around 270 members.

With so many corkscrews in collections and circulation, chances are you will never be caught without one, as W.C. Fields, in the film *My Little Chickadee*, lamented, "Once in the wilds of Afghanistan, I lost my corkscrew, and we were forced to live on nothing but food and water for days."

SEVERAL FISH CORKSCREWS, ONE OF WHICH IS BOTH A CORKSCREW AND LETTER OPENER FASHIONED AS A SWORDFISH

Decanting

Carafe and large cup from Venice and dated around 1860

Opposite: Eighteenth-century wine and liquor tag

*Enjoying a glass of wine was not always as easy as
uncorking a bottle, pouring a glass, and sipping.
Step back in the time tunnel and a ritual—even a
mystique—had taken root, but for good reason.
Winemaking then wasn't as consistently perfect as it
is today. Drinking up back then required more than
a little preparation of the wine.*

Today we tend to decant only older wines, especially very
old reds that throw off sediment and grain as they age in the
bottle. If poured directly into a wine glass, the gathered sediment is stirred up and can muddy and ruin the wine, a nasty
faux pas of the highest degree, and an expensive one. But
when expertly decanted—which involves artfully pouring the
wine into a decanter in a careful fashion that leaves most of
the sediment in the bottle—the fine old wine slips gently
through the bottle's lips and into the decanter, where it catches
its breath before blossoming and inspiring poetry in men.
Sometimes younger wines are decanted simply to give them
a chance to breathe—try it with a very young or rough red.
Often the wine will mellow into something better, more
richly textured, and smoother just by gaining a little air.

But, with many of today's wines, decanting would be more
of an affectation than a practical necessity. It wasn't always so.
Wine was not sold in attractive, labeled bottles until the 19th

SILVER PITCHERS USED DURING MASS SERVICES
IN THE EARLY FOURTEENTH CENTURY

century, nor were vinification techniques as refined as they are today. Decanting was a necessity when wine was sold by the barrel: a butler was dispatched to the cellar where he carefully "canted" the wine for that meal by tapping into a barrel and transferring the wine into a jug, or decanter. Even after bottling at the source of production became more common, the upper classes tended to continue to use decanters, in part because—still—winemaking techniques remained inconsistent (flashforward to, say, the post-World war II era before winemaking began to reach predictable and high levels of consistent purity) and so sediment wasn't uncommon.

A ritual, then and now, decanting required a steady hand, a bit of concentration, and, to the delight of wine accessory collectors, a small battery of special equipment. In keeping with the art of wine, these are gorgeous specimens of the artist's craft, rendered primarily in silver and crystal, that will continue to sparkle on any twenty-first century table.

Decanters

The good news is that there are many decanters and wine jugs that date back to the 17th century— but the bad news is that these beautiful antiques are in museum collections. These include early Venetian glass, Roman glass decanters from the days of the vast Roman Empire (which was responsible for spreading the art of glassmaking across the continent), pottery jugs (which largely replaced glass once the Roman Empire fell, and continued to be popular in the 16th and 17th centuries, with the finest ones mounted with silver or gold handles). Silver, brass, and pewter pitchers reigned in the Middle Ages. The factories on the island of Murano (just a canal away from Venice and a center of glassmaking dating back to 1291, when it was declared an industrial zone centered around glass) fired up its furnaces in the early Renaissance, making Venetian glass the most highly prized ornament across Europe. Glassmaking expanded to other countries in the following centuries and in 1673, England's George Ravenscroft discovered lead crystal (also called flynt glass), which allowed for the production of a heavier, crystal wine jug that could be cut much as a faceted jewel. Introducing lead into the mix made glass stronger and clearer than ever before. Today, some people have become a bit squeamish about lead in their drinking vessels, but Ravenscroft's invention was hailed as a miracle.

For all practical purposes, decanters for today's wine collector begin with the eighteenth century and continue into the nineteenth. The majority of decanters from this period were made to hold a sin-

PORTUGESE CARAFE DATED
TO THE MID-NINETEENTH
CENTURY

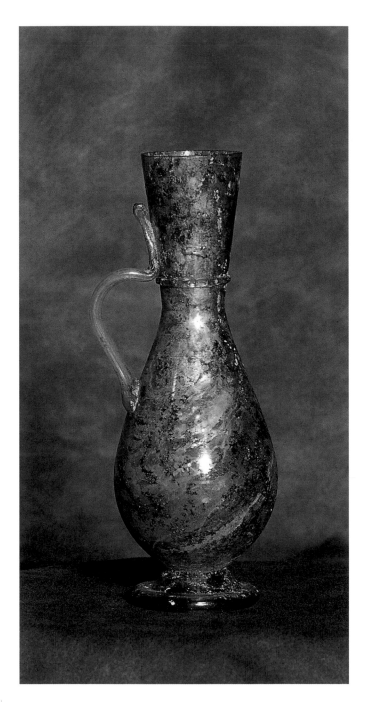

CARAFE DATED TO THE
SIXTH CENTURY A.D.

gle bottle of wine, with room to breathe; those designed to hold magnums are rarer, and thus more valuable. Crystal decanters reflect the advancements in glassmaking, and mirror the style of wine-drinking glasses of their day. Basically, the decanter's form of the last 250 years looks similar to what we use today.

There were an abundance of glass factories in Ireland, producing fine examples (think of Waterford, with its elegant, yet heavy, crystal decanters). Late eighteenth-century examples are simply decorated. In the nineteenth century, steam power was introduced to the cutter's wheels, resulting in deeper and sharper designs known as diamonds, strawberry diamonds, edge cutting, and fan cut rims.

One particular area of collectors' interest is the silver-mounted claret jug, popular in Britain during the Victorian era, reaching its highpoint of popularity in the last quarter of the nineteenth century. Claret (the British term used for red Bordeaux wine) was and remains a favorite in London and claret jugs quickly became quite elaborate, with silver handles replicating climbing vines, holding clear or colored glass jugs, elaborately cut, or engraved with Greek revival scenes, or acid etched.

Some of the most collectible pieces are the more whimsical ones of vessels as animal characters. With bodies of glass and heads of silver, charming jugs were inspired by owls, alligators, fish, and monkeys, among others. Consider the Crichton jug—crafted by artisan Alexander Crichton in 1882, it features a decent likeness of a crested cockatoo (complete with gilded feathers). Excellent examples of this and other antique claret

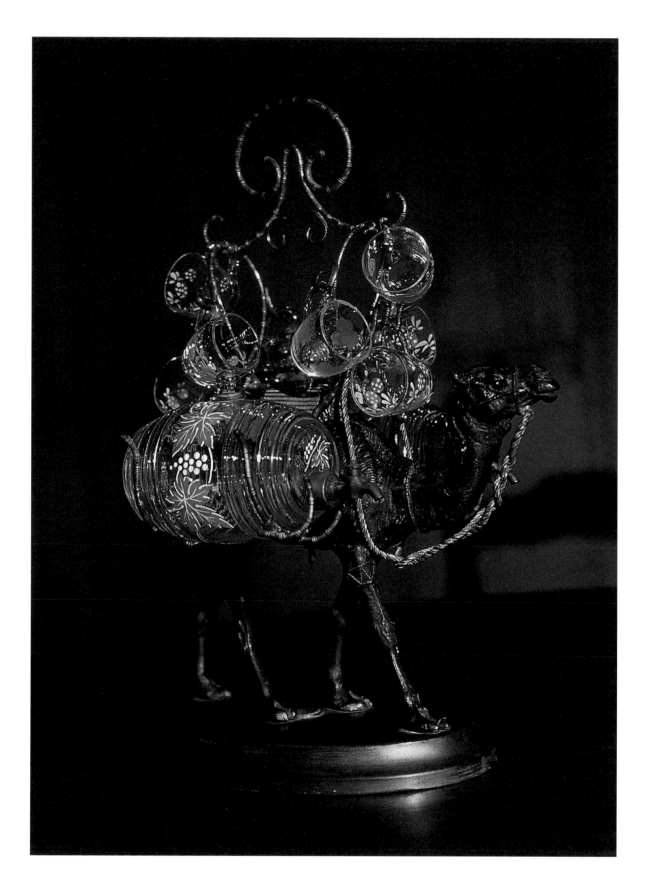

THIS CAMEL, CARRYING
EIGHT GLASSES AND TWO
CONTAINERS FOR LIQUOR,
WAS MADE IN FRANCE
AT THE END OF THE
NINETEENTH CENTURY.

jugs from 1835-1920 are part of The Kent Collection.

While decanters rapidly became objects of great fun—and beauty, in many cases—artists soon turned additional attention to other accoutrements involved in this delicate airing out of wine. Case in point: hallmarked silver wine funnels, which also help ensure the wine is gently transferred from the bottle into the waiting decanter without spilling a precious drop, are hot collectibles due to their boldly striking shapes. A plain funnel could have done this job but when it came to wine, design tended to carry the day and funnels typically were designed to match the silverware.

Wine funnels—almost always featuring a built-in screen to catch impurities—were widely used in the mid-eighteenth century (the earliest known funnel made expressly for wine dates to 1760). Made in silver, the tip of the spout angled so that the wine flows softly against the side wall of the decanter, rather than splashing into the decanter in an upsetting fashion. The strainer is decoratively pierced in geometric patterns to catch the finer residue or cork bits that may float through from the bottle. Some strainers go one step further with a detachable rim that allows for a fine piece of muslin to be laid across for finer filtering. When the heavier sediment appears in the strainer basket, decanting stops and the residue is left in the bottle.

Coasters

In the mid-eighteenth century, wine stains were every bit the nuisance that they are today. Ever resourceful artisans solved this

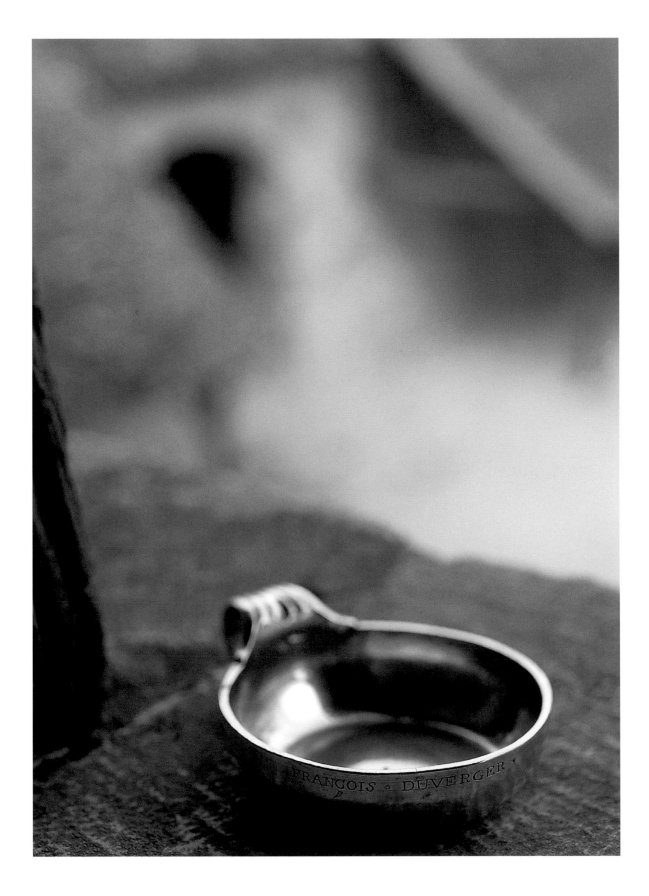

TASTEVIN ENGRAVED
"FRANCOIS DUVERGER,"
MADE IN ORLEANS
BETWEEN 1774 AND 1780

messy issue by creating yet another beautiful accessory, the wine coaster. Once a wine was carefully decanted into a crystal decanter, it was set onto a coaster to protect the table or cloth from wine stains. This high-sided, circular tray was made of silver, gold, or lacquered papier mache. The circumference followed the evolution of the wine decanter. As decanters' size increased to hold a magnum of wine, so the coasters' width expanded to accommodate the wider girths.

Most coasters, however, were made to fit a single-bottle decanter, and they were popular items until the mid-nineteenth century. Today there's a renaissance in the use of wine coasters—both to protect against those stains and for the sheer elegance of the coasters on a table—but usually we use the coaster to hold a bottle, not a decanter. No matter: antique coasters typically perform this job well and an antique coaster is an elegant way to bring a period piece to the table for everyday use. After all, vintage coasters may be used for their original purpose, unlike an older, delicate corkscrew, which may break on uncorking one of today's sturdier bottle corks.

There are stunning examples in antique silver, particularly the positively lovely eighteenth-century Georgian coasters. Sold singly or sometimes in pairs or sets of four or more, these coasters have elaborately pierced sides with a gadrooned or beaded and pierced rim, or perhaps a shell border. The base of the coaster can be silver (engraved with a coat of arms or a design), all wood or wood with crested bosses, or lined with cobalt glass. Some have green baize or felt, possibly old, possibly added

MODERN VESSEL
MADE BY KOSTA
BODA IN SWEDEN

later, on the bottom to prevent table scratches.

If price is of no concern, look for a set of George III silver-gilt wine coasters, crafted by renowned silversmith Benjamin Smith, which might set you back more than the cost of a wine-filled cellar. But there are others in the low thousands, by the silversmith team of Robert and David Hennell, or Philip Rundell, for example, and still other less elaborate silver coasters waiting to be plucked for mere hundreds of dollars.

Lacquered papier-mache models were less expensive then, but rare to find in good condition today. These tend to be gold decoration handpainted on either black or red backgrounds, and are quite decorative.

The Victorian era developed many specialized accoutrements for the table, one of the more preposterous being the coaster wagon or boat. Resembling a toy wagon, albeit in silver or gilt, two coasters were hinged together in a cart on wheels, complete with a handle, so that guests could roll the wine from one guest to the next, circulating the wine themselves if the servants were otherwise occupied.

Bottle Tickets

Today's paper labels on wine bottles not only give the history and provenance of a wine, but many are so decorative that they become conversation pieces. Witness Chateau Mouton Rothschild which, since 1945 has commissioned a different fine artist each year to design the art for the top portion of its

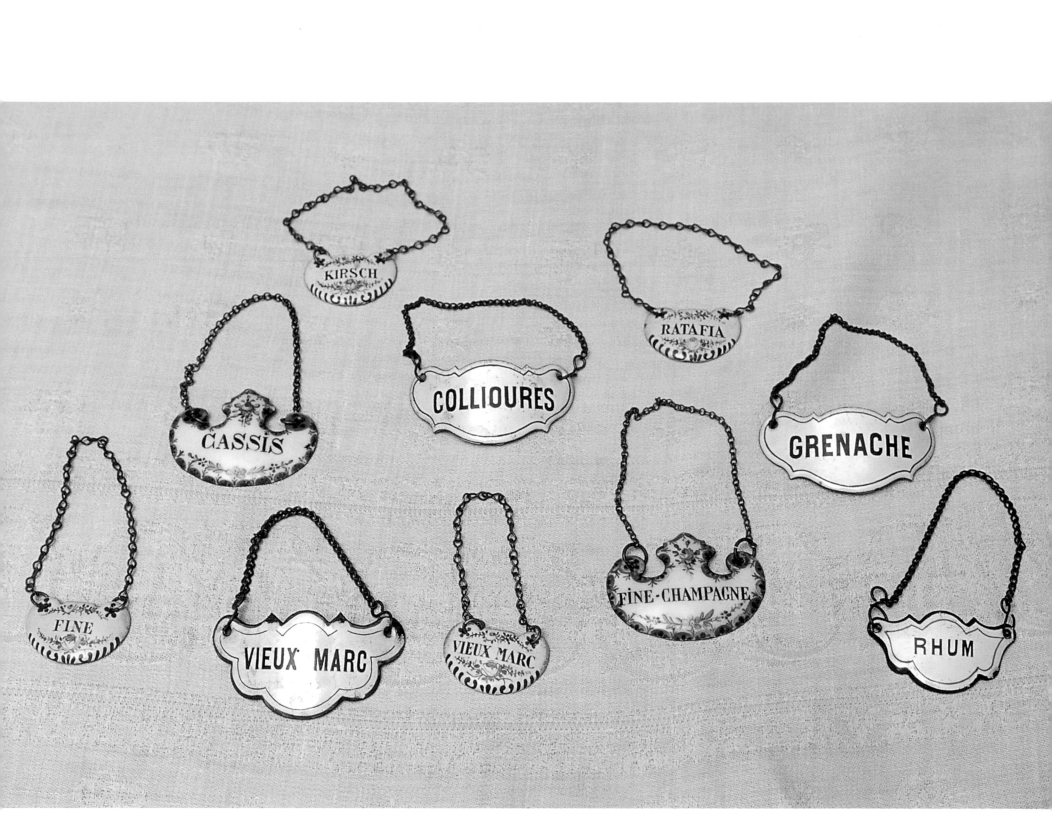

AN ASSORTMENT OF
EIGHTEENTH CENTURY
WINE AND LIQUOR TAGS

label. They've tapped Picasso, Chagall, Dali, Francis Bacon and other artistic notables.

Paper labels didn't exist in the eighteenth century, the golden age of drinking. As all wine was decanted to serve at table, how was the claret to be distinguished from the Madeira? Thus developed, around 1730, the tradition of draping little silver or enamel ID necklaces around the neck of a decanter, clearly spelling out the contents. The popular wines of the era can be noted in the tags that were produced, which included Claret, Hermitage, Madeira, Port, Graves, Hock (Rhine wine), Sauternes, White Wine, Sherry or Brandy. Spelling however was more random than today, and some of the most coveted examples for collectors are those that are misspelled.

The early wine labels, sometimes called bottle tickets, were simple, understated affairs. A thin piece of silver was engraved with the name of the wine, perhaps edged with a brilliant cut to reflect the evening's candlelight, and molded to lay flat against a decanter. The Regency Period introduced

ASSORTED TASTEVINS FROM THE EIGHTEENTH CENTURY

FROM THE COLLECTION OF CHATEÂU DU COLS DE VOUGEOT

bolder shapes, sometimes gilded, illustrating Lilliputian-size scenes of grand Bacchanalian affairs, accented with undulating garlands and grapevines pregnant with fruit. By the Victorian Period, these tiny tableaux of the Machine Age could now be stamped out en masse, allowing for quick and easy production of the most elaborate labels. The wine label was released from its geometric frame, taking on the silhouette of an intricately designed grape leaf, with the name of the wine heavily worked amongst the fragile tendrils and vines. This was one of the more popular styles of the period, but certainly not the only choice. Collectors covet bottle tickets embellished with regimental or family crests, part of the middle class Victorian's quest for ever grander displays of wealth.

After 1860, production dwindled with the introduction of labeled wine bottles, although bottle tickets were still used for fortified wines.

Just a Taste

Tastevins (wine tasters), those beribboned and chained shiny, silver cups that clanked

Eighteenth-century wicker wine basket

on the chest of many a sommelier in the heyday of continental restaurants, were more than just jewelry. Today though, tastevins are an infrequent occurrence and are reminders of a more decadent approach to wine tasting.

But, again, a look at history explains how and why these little cups gained popularity. As far back as the fourteenth century, these shallow silver cups served as tiny wine tasters themselves to wine professionals. A medieval wine merchant would tuck his tastevin into his pocket when traveling on buying trips or when tasting wine before purchasing.

The shallow cups *are* usually made of silver or silverplate and generally range from 3 to 5 inches in diameter, with one or two handles, or none at all. Often the owner's name was engraved on the cup, and sometimes a date. Silver was the preferred material because it did not taint the wine, it was durable (imagine carrying a wine glass in your pocket!), and perhaps most important, the bright silver reflected the true color and density of the wine, a godsend when tasting in dark cellars.

While some tastevins are charmingly decorated with bunches of grapes, tousled leaves, serpent-entwined handles, and gadrooned edges, the serious wine regions of Burgundy and Bordeaux developed their own unique shapes and designs. The Bordeaux variety is more of an open cone, while the Burgundian style is cup shaped. Either way, France produces the most tastevins by far, and perhaps that is why we refer to them by their French name. Indeed, there is no English word for this decorative but functional item.

Harvey's Wine Museum in Bristol, England, which displays French silver tastevins from the late seventeenth century to the mid-eighteenth century, as well as *tasses jumelles*, a hinged set of twin cups used for comparing two wines, which can be snapped closed and slipped into one's pocket after the tasting.

Because tastevins were produced for professionals, fewer were made and antique ones are expensive, but they are available in shops and at auctions. A 2¼-inch diameter, seventeenth-century silver wine taster, with two scrolled handles and some decoration, was priced at $2,700 in a London antique shop. At a Sotheby's, London, auction seventeenth-century silver tastevins went for around $1,750. Silver-plated models from the late nineteenth and twentieth centuries will run much less. France continues to produce tastevins, as they are still used in the cellars of Burgundy and have become a symbol of that region.

EARLY TWENTIETH-CENTURY FAN MADE OUT OF COPPER
AND SILVER, ENGRAVED "MOËT & CHANDON"

Octagonal-shaped wine glasses from
Venice, Italy featuring gold engraving.

Opposite: Wine glass used for Rhine Valley wines,
made by Baccarat and introduced during the
International Exhibition in Nancy in 1909.

Wine glasses

An antique wine glass of a certain vintage will not make a bad wine taste good, but it will make a good wine taste better.

The power of glassware is illustrated in Robert Mondavi's decision to switch to Riedel glasses. In October 1989, Georg Riedel, founder of the eponymous crystal, approached Mondavi about using Riedel stemware in his winery. Riedel had created specific glass shapes which he claimed enhanced specific wines. Mondavi thought his idea nonsense—to him, it was the wine itself that had taste and the glass was just a means to the end of drinking the wine.

Riedel, however, was not easily rebuffed. He persisted and at last gained an audience with Mondavi and several other members of the family at their Napa winery. Side by side, they tasted Mondavi wine in the specially designed Riedel glasses and in the winery's standard wine glasses. Mondavi's response was immediate. He called over his assistant and demanded that all the winery's glasses be replaced at once with Riedel.

Flashforward another decade and nowadays there is wide agreement that good glass will indeed enhance the taste of wine. There similarly is agreement that the right glass helps even more—which is why big reds are poured into large glasses that allow plenty of space for the wine to breathe and also why sparkling wines are served in thin flutes that enhance the gaseous

SET OF GLASSES MADE
FOR THE TSAR OF
RUSSIA IN 1906 BY
BACCARAT.

WEDDING CUP

bubbles. Of course you could serve any wine in any glass—but to get the very best experience, choose the right tool and the payback will be heaven on your tongue.

While all of this is the contemporary and widely accepted catechism among wine connoisseurs, it's actually all quite a new doctrine. Indeed, it wasn't until the late eighteenth century that varied shapes of glasses began to appear at the table. Up until then, earlier cultures kept a simpler inventory: a gourd for earliest man, a pottery cup, a golden chalice, silver goblet, footed brass cup or glass sufficed.

Nor were wine glasses lined up like a sparkly battalion in front of each guest's place. That didn't happen until the mid-nineteenth century, when service a la Russe was introduced and diners learned how to pass to the right. A gentleman of previous centuries would have depended on his footman to bring him a glass of wine, which he would drink right down, hand back the glass, and motion when he was ready for another. If he was over-served, it was by his own man. Wine had not reached today's point of complexity or

WINE GLASSES FROM THE RHINE VALLEY INTRODUCED AT THE
INTERNATIONAL EXHIBITION IN NANCY, FRANCE, 1909

finesse that encourages guests to sip and swirl during a meal.

Glass eventually became the most popular material for wine vessels, although it was considered a luxury. For the wealthy merchants of Venice or Europeans of Renaissance high society, Venetian glass was highly prized. The glassmakers on the island of Murano were the Pavarottis of their day, although the Venetian rulers kept them on-island in golden handcuffs, loathe to let any secret of their only major industry leak beyond their shores. Their creations were truly extraordinary—blue, green, purple, and turquoise glass with enameled bowls and vigorous lines. They are extremely rare on the market today. However, Murano continues to produce extraordinary and vibrant wineglasses. These opulent glasses, with contorted dolphins for stems, geometric patterns, luscious ice cream and jewel colors, and fantastical silhouettes are eye candy for the table.

For collectors of antique wine glasses, leave the Renaissance for the Rockefellers and look for glasses from the eighteenth century to fill your shelves, specifically

crystal from the Georgian period.

Quite a few remain from the latter part of the century to hunt down, and they are quite simply the best glass to collect because the British were demanding when it came to the decorative arts. The century's increased wine drinking called for vessels which measured up to their high standards. Some of these will cost more than a bottle of wine, but many will be less than a bottle of Chateau Lafite.

The Politics of Glass

You would not think glass would be highly politicized but, in many ways, it has long been. A first hint is how zealously the Venetian dukes tried to guard the secrets of their Murano glassmakers. But matters became clearer still in 1615 when England passed a proclamation that flatly banned the use of wood in glass furnaces. Why? The countryside was rapidly being denuded of trees in efforts to produce enough glass to slake the nation's thirst. Not exactly environmentalists, the royals weren't trying to curb drinking so much as they wanted to keep the forests for use in England's ship building industry. As a result, glassmaking shifted to regions where coal was plentiful. More important stylistically, however, is that in this early seventeenth century period, monopoly rights to glassmaking were essentially held by one individual, Sir Robert Mansell. After his death in 1656 and the restoration of royalty in 1660, when Charles II took the throne (ending the rule of Oliver Cromwell), the monopoly ended and control of glassmaking shifted to the Worshipful Company of

Glass Sellers, a splendid name for a London guild. That also marked a substantial shift in design philosophy—the guild's members closely monitored their customers' needs and responded accordingly. A flowering of English glassmaking followed—and this was cranked into high gear by George Ravenscroft, who figured out a way to make lead crystal around 1675. He made this discovery under prodding from the guild which wanted a more durable glass and, by adding lead oxide into the glass mix, he succeeded beyond the guild's wildest hopes. Not only was Ravenscroft crystal as rugged as Venice's, it—to most eyes—had superior brilliance. When light hits this kind of crystal, it not only sparkles but it seems to dance—the visual effects are quite spectacular and, accordingly, home-blown glass soon became the rage in England.

The British Collectibles

Factor in durability with popularity and, for collectors, what this means is that there remain many examples of English glasswares from the seventeenth and eighteenth centuries. Thanks to Ravenscroft, these glasses are quite heavy, which also made them suitable for cut and engraved decoration.

Arriving on the scene around 1710, the baluster—which replicated the balustrades then popular in architecture and furniture—quickly became the most popular glass. Like many glasses of the period it has a folded foot—a rather menacing term indicating that the glass's foot is literally folded over at its bottom, adding more solidity to the base.

FLERS 1909 SERIES, INTRODUCED AT THE INTERNATIONAL EXHIBITION IN NANCY, FRANCE, 1909

BOHEME 1860

Balusters became balustroids after 1745, due to a tax levied on glassmakers, imposed mainly to raise cash for the state. Glassmakers responded by lightening up and doing the twist. They changed their formula to a lighter weight glass, and heavy balusters became lighter balustroids, with plainer decoration except for the stem. They also incorporated air twist stems—a rather nifty technique that creates clear or milky white (called an opaque twist) swirls in the stem, resembling a double helix corkscrew. This cut down on the amount of glass used—and thus the tax—but also produced some of the period's most desired collectibles.

Curiously, although quite eye-catching, glasses with different color stems simply never caught on, at least not in England. Color twists were known to have been made as early as 1760, but only a handful of glasses remain—all breathtakingly valuable because of the rarity. Funny because, in the later eighteenth century, they were nearly impossible to give away. Nobody wanted this multi-toned glass and they languished on shelves.

Meantime, another upshot of the 1745 Excise Tax was that much glassmaking shifted to Ireland—think Waterford crystal—which was exempt from the levy. If Irish industry needed a shot in the arm, this tax loophole provided it and Ireland, although primarily aping British styles, soon became a major producer of fine glasswares, most of which were exported to Britain or the U.S.

The eighteenth century also saw the birth of a delightful design technique—stippling, invented by German glassmaker Anna Roemers, and quickly adopted in England, which involved using a kind of pointillism to create images on glass. By making countless tiny dots on the glass, images took shape—and so glassware flowered with horses, fish, birds, children, and just about any imaginable form.

As the eighteenth century flowed forward, engraving became quite the thing—and even doubled back to embrace political themes. The central issue in early eighteenth-century British politics was the struggle between supporters of the Catholic Stuarts (so-called Jacobeans, they favored Charles II and his kin) and the Protestant supporters of William of Orange (who became king in 1688). Jacobeans often drank from glasses engraved with an open rose, to show the flowering of the Catholic monarchy. Supporters of William of Orange preferred to drink from glasses engraved with a figure of William on horseback. While such glasses are believed to have been plentiful, do note: Original glassware with any of these symbols is extremely valuable, but forgeries are epidemic. Worse, many forgeries, apparently, were the result of engraving on genuine Georgian glass—which makes detection a tricky piece of business. For most collectors, the prohibitive prices of these engraved glasses (well upwards of $10,000 per) and the high risks, make this type of collectible impossible to collect. Look at the Jacobean (the rose engraved) and the Williamite (equestrian) engravings in museums but leave the collecting to well-endowed institutions.

A last Georgian trend: painted glassware. Developed to its highest form by an artist named William Beilby—who worked around Newcastle-upon-Tyne, where coal to fuel his glass furnaces was plentiful—this technique saw enamel paintings fused with an underlying glass to produce genuine, if miniature, works of art. Perhaps his most notable work was a glass commissioned by a wealthy tradesman, Edward Charlton of Hesleyside, who wanted a glass that would hold a full bottle of claret. Beilby responded with a massive goblet. On one side was inscribed, The Standard of Hesleyside. On the reverse is the Charlton family coat of arms. Supposedly, it soon became the custom for visitors to be challenged to grasp the gob-

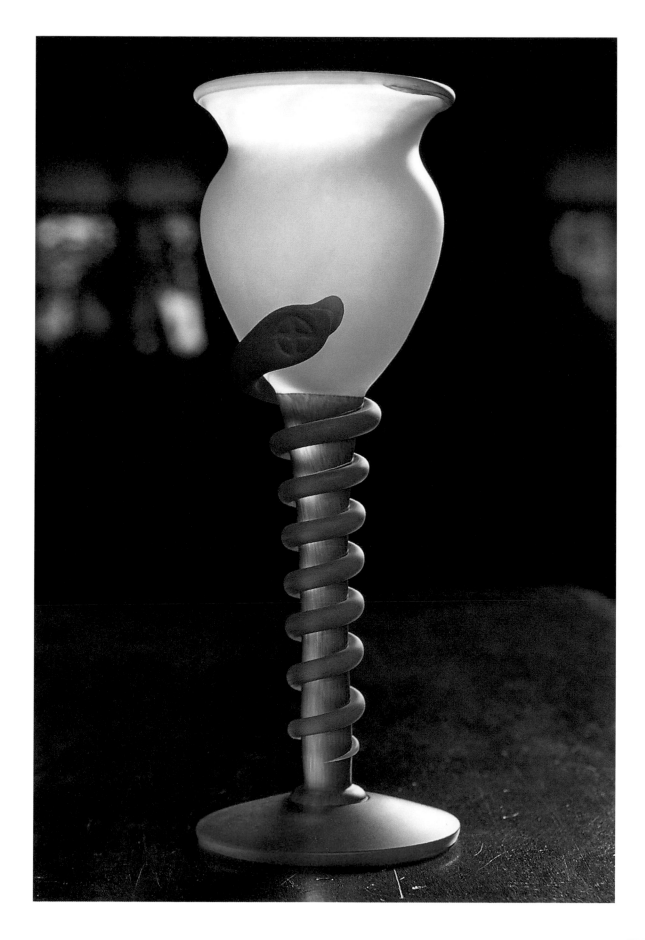

let and, in a single, long swallow, down its contents without taking a breath!

Alas, Beilby's Standard of Hesleyside goblet was damaged by Charlton's drunken butler, but many other Beilby glasses remain and their range is remarkable: hunting scenes, ancient monuments, and many with family crests and coats of arms.

Although paintings on glass—even cameos, which gained popularity in the Victorian era—had their day in wine glass design, for the most part things settled down and centered around clear glassware, all the better to see the wine that was about to be drunk.

Glassmaking continued apace for a century or so but, come the late nineteenth century, the next, new and big thing detonated in the design arena: art nouveau, birthed in Central Europe, and with it came delectable glasses of multiple tones. A glass might, for instance, have a clear stem and a deeply, dark green bowl, or perhaps a ruby red bowl. Given the monotones of most of the stemware that had gained favor in Northern Europe for several centuries, these art nouveau glasses made for an instantly striking appearance in the hand or on the table. The finest varieties are usually thought to have been made by Czechs in and around Prague, but everywhere in middle Europe art nouveau glass production found favor.

Meantime, another force was gaining strength in glassmaking and—by the twentieth century—it reigned supreme: a push for absolutely faultless crystal. Designs became ever simpler, but manufacturing techniques became ever more sophisticated. An irony is that today's best crystal—say, Riedel's Sommelier line which is made in limited quantities for use by restaurants and hotels—now actually costs more than nineteenth century (and sometimes even older) glass. The Riedel Sommelier Bordeaux Grand Cru, a sumptuous glass capable of holding 30 ounces, retails for upwards of $60, per stem. A keen shopper with an eye for bargains often can turn up good quality eighteenth-century glassware for under $50 per stem or a turn of the century art nouveau stem for perhaps $25. Which is better? Here, as with most things antique or gastronomic, there simply is no disputing taste. But, for certain, a sip of wine from an elegant glass—be it brand new or an antique—just somehow does taste that much better.

Rhine Valley wine glass introduced at the 1909
International Exhibition in Nancy, France

Crystal glass with ruby tint made in Bohemia
at the end of the nineteenth century;
it's engraved with a castle from the Rhine Valley.

La beauté extra
ordinaire
De ce gobelet
d'argent
Le rend pour vous
digne d'y faire
Ce qu'il ne fit
jamais avant
D'y boire un cham
pagne si bon
D'y boire un Moët
et Chandon

S P

Wine coolers

Ice bucket by Moët & Chandon in a boiled carton dating to 1930

Opposite: Silver champagne cup made by Moët & Chandon

Do any of us dare remember what it was like before Frigidaire? Could a Muscadet ever get cold enough to wash down briny oysters? And where would ice cubes come from to chill the water that slowly chills the bottle of Riesling we expect to have with the duck liver pate?

It's just not part of our realm. But it was reality for the hostesses and hosts who had to entertain in grand style in earlier centuries, impeccably dressed with no air conditioning to save them from layers of clothing. With wine drinking becoming increasingly popular in the late eighteenth and early nineteenth centuries, it was once again the artists who responded to the call, this time of how to chill a wine with style.

Perhaps the most impressive of these creations, and certainly an extravagant item today, is the silver wine cistern and fountain ensemble. Just the name sounds daunting, but coming face to face with one of the more enticing examples, still functioning just as smoothly as if we had time-traveled back 300 years, is proof enough that this is the holy grail for the wine collector who has had his fill of wine coasters.

This imposing *pièce de résistance* would have been centerstage at the most formal banquets, perhaps an emperor or king, surely statesmen or their footmen, all took their turn at one of the spigots that delivered chilled wine. Not only is it a showpiece, but useful for chilling wines as well as dispensing wine,

MODERN DISPOSABLE
CHAMPAGNE BUCKET
MADE OF CARDBOARD

or sparkling wine. When emptied and not being employed in a grand fete, this wine accessory makes a major statement about how you feel about wine simply by sitting there.

One of the most famous of these was recently auctioned at Christie's. It was a royal silver cistern and fountain ensemble commissioned in Germany (maker's mark of Lewin Dedeke) around 1710 by the Elector of Hanover. Its provenance is impeccable. Who ever heard of The Elector, you may ask, but he was soon after crowned King of England, King George I, and wisely brought the now famous Hanover cistern and fountain with him to London. The silver remained in the royal family until it was sold to newspaper magnate William Randolph Hearst in 1924. Said cistern was later acquired by a private owner, who sold it at Christie's which in turn auctioned it to an anonymous buyer for $1.3 million.

Tabletop Wine Coolers

One look at a William IV silver wine cooler, or cistern as it was sometimes called, in the very regal campagna style with twin, upturned handles and fat-bellied buckets, rimmed with luminous, silver encrusted leaves, and chilling a bottle of wine in the sink will instantly lose all appeal. Chilling down a wine is simply another excuse to cart out the Georgian and Victorian silver.

Wine coolers in the Regency style will positively blind guests with their ornateness. Not only are the buckets ormolu, but embossed with lyrical tales of the Greek Revival. Golden gods and goddesses pose in their chariot as Dionysus's head sprouts handles as if devil's horns, and acanthus leaves and grape leaves envelope the bowl. Once chilled, the characters appear to perspire as the bucket frosts. Is Greece really so warm, or Olympus so heated with the gods' constant bickering? Who's to know from these elaborate scenes, wrought in gold as bright as the Grecian sun?

Other Georgian silver coolers are made of silver, with curious heads peering from beneath trailing grapevines entwined just below the rim, and uplifting gadrooning at the base, all inviting one to the enjoyment of wine before the bottle has even been opened.

A somewhat simpler George II wine cooler is bold in its shining silver, sand pail-shaped silhouette, sporting solely a giant, regal coat of arms between the gadrooned base and rim.

These coolers are often found in pairs and make an outstanding statement as twin towers on the sideboard, where they would have belonged in days of yore. No candlesticks could possibly draw as much attention, or lend a room as much character as a sin-

MOULIN ROUGE SERIES
CHAMPAGNE BUCKET,
CIRCA 1960

gle pair of these fully functional items, necessary to the lifestyle of any wine enthusiast.

At what price? Christie's has auctioned off Regency-era silver wine coolers (crafted by artisan Paul Storr) for $10,000 to $20,000 and the probability of obtaining one of these for under $10,000 is a fantasy. A touch of good news is that, lately, silver-plate knock-offs of classic table-top coolers are hitting the market, usually with prices under $1,000. Inquire at any retailer of better silver and silver plate. Admittedly, that price tag is a far cry above the $25 or so fetched by the high-tech, acrylic chillers that are increasingly popular in restaurants—but whoever would use a chunk of plastic as a table's centerpiece? These acrylic units may work—in fact, do work, well—but not only are they ugly today, they will be similarly ugly in the next century. Save your pennies and wait to buy a silver-plate replica of a grand, old chiller because then you have something worth looking at.

Cellarettes

Many of us dream of assembling a wine cellar one day, but wouldn't it be swell to have a cellarette in the meantime? These portable units for chilling wine were the doll furniture of their time. If you couldn't quite afford a dining table by the renowned cabinet maker Duncan Phyfe, perhaps you could purchase a cellarette designed by him, with all the same lines, motifs, craftsmanship, and lustrous wood for which his furniture was famous.

Both American and English cabinetmakers jumped into the wine scene by designing cellarettes in keeping with the design style of the day. Wealthy households would certainly have had at least one, possibly tucked under the sideboard in the dining room, and probably of a style that complemented their dining room furniture. These were made of mahogany, sometimes banded with brass, other times carved and ornamented. Cellarettes came in oval, rectangular, or hexagonal shapes, with brass handles on the side. Some are elevated on narrow legs that taper to brass castors, perfect for mobility. Roll out this handsome antique at your next dinner party and it will elevate the status of whatever wine rests inside. Those of the Regency period mimicked sarcophagus shapes and were built low to the ground, crouching on heavily carved claw feet.

Lined with lead or zinc, they would have been filled with iced water and just over a case-worth of wine bottles would have been slipped in to chill for the extensive meal to come. The dimensions of the cellarettes changed to keep up with the evolving shape of the wine bottle, becoming deeper later in the eighteenth century to accommodate taller bottles, keeping

1878 CELLARETTE INTRODUCED AT THE
PARIS UNIVERSAL EXHIBITION, 1878

them up to their necks in water and, for many of the models, shut smartly with a wooden cover.

If planning to use one of these for chilling wine, do make sure the tin lining is still leakproof. Most should have a tap for draining the water, as well.

Monteiths

Around 1670, someone had the idea to chill wine glasses before serving chilled wine. In days before central air, a glass of cold, cold wine on a hot, hot day must have been a thrilling proposition. Not only was it practical, keeping the beverage chilled and the guest cool a bit longer, but it was yet another decorative focal point, and ritual, for the host. For this purpose, a monteith was used, sometimes called a wine glass cooler or rinser, and they remained popular for about 40 years. Word is that a Scotsman of wild reputation, known for the scalloped hem of his cape, was the eponymous source for this elegant cooler. Whatever the inspiration, the monteith as cooler was a gener-ous-sized oval or round bowl, often with lions' mask handles on either side, with a scalloped rim which held 10–12 wine glasses by their feet, allowing their bowls to be plunged into the chilling liquid.

Silver punchbowls of the late seventeenth century sometimes doubled as wine glass coolers, and some were smartly outfitted with detachable, circular notched rims that could be fitted over the top of the bowl, converting it to a monteith. This dual-purpose instrument must have seemed very modern at the time.

Nonetheless, monteiths developed into their own, becoming one impressively wrought piece fashioned out of silver, gilt-edged porcelain, pewter, brass and toleware. Antique ones can be prohibitive in cost: a blue and white Dutch delft monteith in perfect con-dition was snapped up at a recent auction for just under $10,000. It would be stylish today to chill mar-tini glasses in such an antique, or let it shine on its own cool self, sans water, as a centerpiece. These perfect antiques really need nothing more than admiration.

MERCIER ICE BUCKET FOR QUARTER BOTTLES

Bottle stoppers

Left: Mercier advertising poster featuring
the Geffard gas balloon at the 1878 Paris World Fair.

Above: Glass stopper made by Stephano Morasso in Venice, Italy

If you're now convinced you want to be a collector of wine antiques, but think your budget won't let you into the game, there is good news. Cultivate a love for bottle stoppers and for well under $100, you're into a niche field in the world of wine accessories. Bottle stoppers are easy enough to find, not exorbitantly expensive, and their small size allows you to amass a respectable collection without adding another room to your house, or taking out a bank loan. Even a small collection can have great charm and be shown to advantage when inserted into a lineup of wine bottles selected for an evening's dinner party.

Besides their affordability and availability, many of these little stoppers enjoy their own charismatic qualities, ranging from the simple to the positively amusing. Stoppers were made in Europe and North America in the early twentieth century as a way to re-cork bottles of wine and other spirits once the original cork had been pulled. Their usefulness is evident if you've ever had a cork break or crumble as it is pulled from the bottle, or if you've tried to cram an expanded cork back into the bottle. They continue to be produced to this day, and some sport metal or glass stoppers, but the older ones were generally made of tapered cork or porcelain, topped with carved and painted ornamentation. The decorative tops are what interest the col-

lector. Hand-carved wood stoppers from the early 1900s tend to focus on human and animal characters, but by the end of the century, there wasn't anything a manufacturer couldn't mass-produce on the tiny circumference of a cork top: wine and cheese platters, whole lobsters, sailing boats, golf balls, doctors with stethoscopes, chefs holding cleavers, likenesses of famous politicians, lighthouses, train engines—the inch-wide field was wide open.

Especially whimsical as a focused collection are the early German mechanical stoppers which feature a cork topped with a 3- to 5½-inch-tall carved wooden motif of a human figure. Each featured a lever on the back. When pulled down or pushed in, the lever would create an action in the character: a man would stick out his tongue and roll his eyes, turn down or open his mouth, take off his hat, raise a bottle to an opening mouth, tilt his head and play the violin, or a couple would turn their heads and kiss. Hand-painted and hand-carved of wood and painted bright, now faded, colors, the faces have wonderful, comical expressions.

A COMPOSITION BULLDOG CORKSCREW AND
STOPPER SET, AND A SILVER BULLDOG STOPPER
(WHICH IS A SHEATH FOR THE WORM)

A MODERN LAZY FISH BOTTLE STOPPER

Other kinetic stoppers on the market have a ball and string (later replaced by monofilament line) which, when pulled, activates the motion. These are delightful toys in themselves with finely detailed handwork.

The Germans expressed a sense of humor in their bottle stoppers. Later porcelain examples feature ridiculous-looking little animals hand-painted in the wildest colors. Hippos and rhinos are a favorite theme, their plump bodies given lavender stripes, pink or blue polka dots, orange or green leopard spots, or tiny frogs with eyes wide open who ride on their backs. Other wacky porcelain animals include a yellow chicken with a white kerchief, 24-carat gold and blue snail, which also comes with those hand-painted leopard spots, a quacking duck, and chubby fish.

One of the larger producers of stoppers from 1912–1976 was an Italian company, Anri. They made both human and animal figures, some with movable parts, some just the head and others full-figure, which became popular souvenir items after World War I. Seek out these early ones which

CHAMPAGNE BOTTLE SEALERS

STOPPER MADE OUT OF PEWTER

SILVER BULLDOG STOPPER WHICH SERVES AS A SHEATH FOR THE WORM

were hand-carved. The human figures were fashioned after the villagers themselves, who carved them and included all the quirky, individual facial features they saw in faces around them. As mass production later took over, the expressions and faces became standardized and much of the charm was lost.

Some stoppers allow for the liquid to be poured through the cork and top, without removing the stopper from the bottle. These are called bottle stopper pourers. European examples feature painted ceramic heads of jolly, red-cheeked men or women villagers, all wearing hats placed at jaunty angles atop their hairstyles. Tip the bottle and the liquid pours through the top of the hat.

All sorts of metal examples are on the market. Old English brass bottle stoppers can be found topped with Dickens' characters, such as Mr. Pickwick. A Belgian one replicates the Mannequin Pee in the Grand Place of Brussels. Silver, silverplate, and pewter stoppers are favorites for animal heads. Cast metal heads are fashioned in likenesses of pirates, Turks, monks, Scotsmen, and Russians, as well as likenesses of J.F.K., Kruschev,

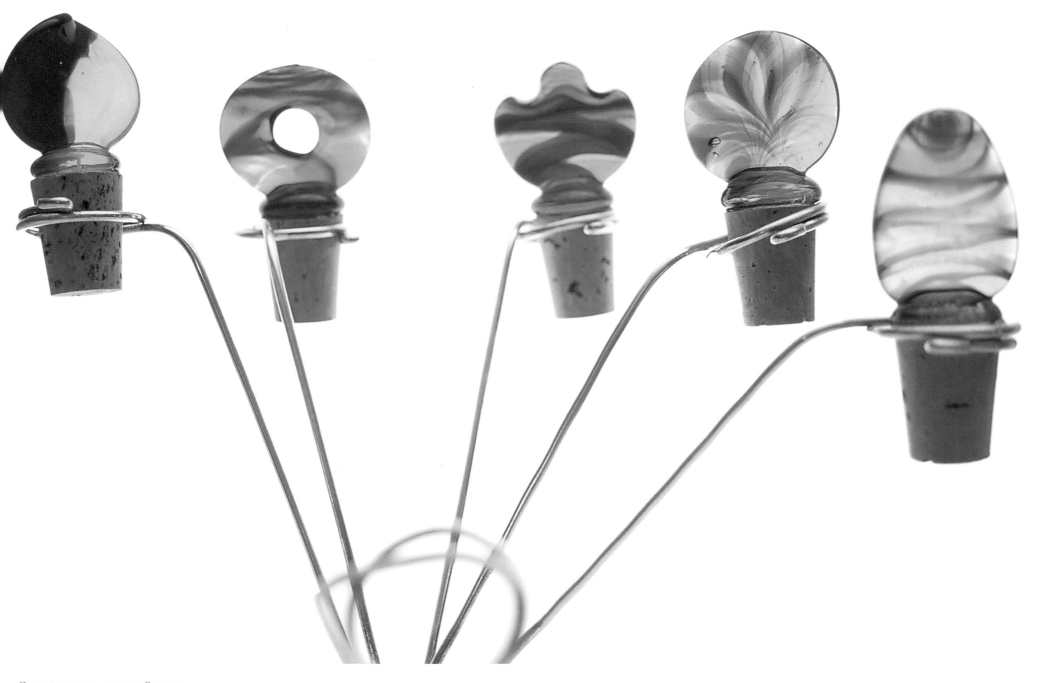

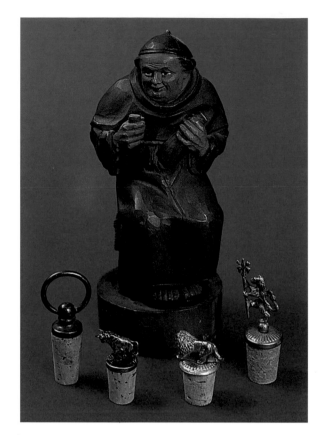

favorite pal, Bimbo the dog. She's decorative too, posing in Santa, waitress, golfing, tennis, Monroe, and Cowgirl costumes.

What might a stopper fetch? Surveys of e-Bay and offline auctions found vintage stoppers selling for anywhere from $10 to $25 apiece. That's why even a small investment can yield a significant collection—and it's also why a collector needs a strategy because, at these prices, it's very easy to buy and keep buying. One strategy: focus on a country and a time-period, for instance, early twentieth-century German stoppers. Within fairly short order, you'll acquire both significant expertise—and an eye-catching collection.

Years from now, bottle stoppers might just become the hottest collectible, and your comprehensive collection could show up on the auction block, yielding a princely sum. Or not. Engage in collecting because you love the hunt, have a passion for the art object that has become your *premier amour*, and for the joy of looking at and sharing your collection, and knowledge, with others. As a collector, there's always the risk of becoming somewhat ever more pathological, be it about German bottle stoppers, French corkscrews or Edwardian silver wine coolers. You will know you have joined the collectors' ranks when more is never enough. There will always be one more piece you will have to have.

and Britain's former Prime Minister Harold Wilson.

Often you'll find bottle stoppers sold in sets, and occasionally a set will include a corkscrew and bottle opener, each with a similar carved motif or theme. Many stoppers also came with attached chains and rings that could be placed over the bottle, keeping the stopper attached to the bottle when uncorked.

One of the more recognizable personalities to ever cork a wine is Betty Boop. The flirtatious Betty keeps wine air tight with her perfect gams firmly planted atop the cork, sometimes assisted by her